C A P S T O N E

C000185423

Stay Smart!

Smart things to know about… is a complete library of the world's smartest business ideas. **Smart** books put you on the inside track to the knowledge and skills that make the most successful people tick.

Each book brings you right up to speed on a crucial business issue. The subjects that business people tell us they most want to master are:

Smart Things to Know about **Brands & Branding**, JOHN MARIOTTI

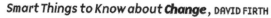
Smart Things to Know about **Business Finance**, KEN LANGDON

Smart Things to Know about **Change**, DAVID FIRTH

Smart Things to Know about **Customers**, ROS JAY

Smart Things to Know about **Decision Making**, KEN LANGDON

Smart Things to Know about **E-Commerce**, MIKE CUNNINGHAM

Smart Things to Know about **Innovation & Creativity**, DENNIS SHERWOOD

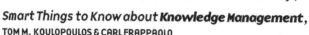
Smart Things to Know about **Knowledge Management**,
TOM M. KOULOPOULOS & CARL FRAPPAOLO

Smart Things to Know about **Managing Projects**, DONNA DEEPROSE

Smart Things to Know about **Marketing**, JOHN MARIOTTI

Smart Things to Know about **Partnerships**, JOHN MARIOTTI

Smart Things to Know about **People Management**, DAVID FIRTH

Smart Things to Know about **Strategy**, RICHARD KOCH

Smart Things to Know about **Teams**, ANNEMARIE CARACCIOLO

Smart Things to Know about **Your Career**, JOHN MIDDLETON

You can stay **Smart** by e-mailing us at **info@wiley-capstone.co.uk**
Let us keep you up to date with new Smart books, Smart updates, a Smart newsletter
and Smart seminars and conferences. Get in touch to discuss your needs.

CAPSTONE

Smart

THINGS TO KNOW ABOUT ...

People
Management

DAVID FIRTH

First published 2001 by
Capstone Publishing Ltd (A John Wiley & Sons Co.)
8 Newtec Place
Magdalen Road
Oxford OX4 1RE
United Kingdom
http://www.capstoneideas.com

British Library Cataloguing in Publication Data
A CIP catalogue record for this book is available from the British Library

ISBN 1-84112-073-1

Typeset by
Forewords, 109 Oxford Road, Cowley, Oxford
Printed and bound by
T.J. International Ltd, Padstow, Cornwall

This book is printed on acid-free paper

People are bloody ignorant apes
    Waiting for Godot, Samuel Beckett

You are peace and joy and light.
    Conversations with God, Neil Donald Walsch

I have ever hated all Nations, professions and Communities, and all my love is towards individuals; . . . principally I hate and detest that animal called Man, although I hartily love John, Peter, Thomas and so forth.
    Correspondence, Jonathan Swift

Contents

What is Smart?

The *Smart* series *is* a new way of learning. *Smart* books will improve your understanding and performance in some of the critical areas you face to-day like *customers, strategy, change, e-commerce, brands, influencing skills, knowledge management, finance, teamworking, partnerships.*

Smart books summarize accumulated wisdom as well as providing original cutting-edge ideas and tools that will take you out of theory and into action.

The widely respected business guru Chris Argyris points out that even the most intelligent individuals can become ineffective in organizations. Why? Because we are so busy working that we fail to learn about ourselves. We stop reflecting on the changes around us. We get sucked into the patterns of behavior that have produced success for us in the past, not realizing that it may no longer be appropriate for us in the fast-approaching future.

There are three ways the *Smart* series helps prevent this happening to you:

- by increasing your self-awareness

- by developing your understanding, attitude and behavior

- by giving you the tools to challenge the status quo that exists in your organization.

Smart people need smart organizations. You could spend a third of your career hopping around in search of the Holy Grail, or you could begin to create your own smart organization around you today.

Finally a reminder that books don't change the world, people do. And although the *Smart* series offers you the brightest wisdom from the best practitioners and thinkers, these books throw the responsibility on you to *apply* what you're learning in your work.

Because the truly smart person knows that reading a book is the start of the process and not the end . . .

As Eric Hoffer says, "In times of change, learners inherit the world, while the learned remain beautifully equipped to deal with a world that no longer exists.'

David Firth
Smartmaster

Preface

Lots of management books tell you what to do. They give you the techniques and tools that are traditionally associated with the art of management.

This book tells you *why* to do the things you might choose to do as a manager.

It advocates that you are people centred, not technique centred, that your behaviour springs from an understanding of human beings, not from a memorisation of procedures and tools.

Why does *Smart Things to Know about People Management* take this stance?

One of the great myths of 20th-century management development was that if you could get the managers and leaders of an organization to think, say and do 'the right things', then everyone would be happy. Global management development is an industry of no small proportions

($58 billion in 1997 in the US alone). But the trouble with just working on what managers should do or practice makes some huge assumptions about the people who are the object of a manager's doing. One assumption is that people are neutral, passive beings and that if you do the right thing, then people will react in just the way the text book indicates. Flick this switch and you turn them on.

Another assumption is that people are blank slates, empty canvases on which the manager paints his or her decisions and actions, empty vessels waiting to be filled by managerial will.

These assumptions do not reflect reality. And the amount of grouching and moaning by managers about their people which goes on in organizations (in exactly the way people grouch and moan about their management), proves that the assumptions do not reflect reality. Managing can be a joy, but it can also be, truly, a bitch. I think we should all acknowledge that.

The reality is that people are hugely unpredictable, complex, inconsistent animals who may or may not react in the way you expect. They are also far from being blank slates – they have all manner of stuff in their heads, most of which is generated from their experiences in the past and by their social development, and most of which – to make matters worse – is largely unconscious to them.

However, there is a practical solution: to isolate some principles by which all human beings seem to work and base your management behaviour around those. And when that fails, learn from it and try something else. Be flexible.

There is also a philosophical approach you can choose to take, when faced with the reality that people are hugely unpredictable, complex, inconsistent animals. The choice you have is neatly summed up by Jonathan Swift, who provides one of the epithets to this book.

Jonathan Swift wrote *Gulliver's Travels*, a book about a man whose mind was so broadened by travel that it snapped like over-stretched elastic. So convinced was Gulliver he had found Utopia, that when he returned home to England to face up to the shortcomings of human beings, he found he could do nothing but hate them. This misanthropic reaction of Gulliver is balanced by Swift's own, who has the wisdom to accept that much of what mankind does could be considered hateful, but not all of it, and not all the time. Swift's own beliefs seemed to be that mankind is capable of being like a beast, and is capable of being like an angel – so don't, he advocates, ever be surprised at either attribute showing up.

There's a huge range of behaviour between beast and angel, of course, most of which many of us traverse every day – and to which managers need to respond.

So what are these 'principles by which all human beings seem to work'? There are many, of course, and you probably have some generated from your personal experience of being human and being among humans. But I've chosen to look at seven.

Each chapter in this book, begins with an essential, 'Smart Thing to Know about People', which has a critical implication for you as a manager.

These Smart Things are:

1 **The principle:** People live in time; mostly the past, hopefully the future and, fleetingly, the present.
   The implication: How can you endeavour to keep people out of the past? What is the history of management and managing that will inform people's perceptions of you?

2 **The principle:** Life is a product of the choices that people make every day.
   The implication: Why would anyone choose to work with you and your company? How can you attract the best talent?

3 **The principle:** People are living human beings.
   The implication: What do they require from organisations today that's different from the past?

4 **The principle:** People are fundamentally creative creatures: people make things mean things through the act communication.
   The implication: What's the best way to connect them together and to you? How can you make things mean what you want them to mean?

5 **The principle:** People are desperate for recognition, acceptance and approval.
   The implication: What's the best way to get things done in your company through giving them those things?

6 **The principle:** Life is difficult.
   The implication: What's the best way to deal with the stresses, strains and shadow side of life in organisations?

7 **The principle:** The future only equals the past if people choose to make it so.
   The implication: How can you keep your company energised, refreshed and pointing in the right direction?

So this book looks at the traditional management tools but from a different angle. It suggests, for example, that you delegate not because managers are supposed to delegate, but with the added understanding that tells you how people respond and grow when they are delegated to. And when you understand what actually goes on when human beings communicate, you will change the way you choose to communicate, and will cease to be frustrated by why you've failed to 'get through to them' in the past.

This people-centred approach, I believe, will help us move a little closer to realising the promise of the old cliché: *our people are our greatest asset*.

I hope you enjoy this book, and that managing becomes for you, well, less of a bitch . . .

1

We May Have Done With the Past, But the Past Has Not Done With Us

> **A Smart Thing to Know about People**
>
> People live in time.
>
> They are haunted by the past, threatened by the future, frustrated by the present.

In this chapter we will examine how management is intimately concerned with the impact of the past on present behaviour.

Managing an organization is like operating a time machine. Your job is to guide it from where it is today to a better place (one characterized by higher revenues, maybe, or greater profits, or larger market share, or sales per head that would make a whore blush, but whatever the measurement, a better place) tomorrow. You take the place from here to there, from the present into the future. The time machine is not completely unusual since it has a manual – this book. It is completely unusual in that its passengers, its engine and its fuel are all combined into one: this substance is called 'your people'.

Unfortunately you have a challenge. People don't embrace the future when they are living in the past.

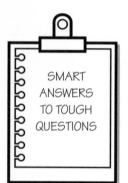

SMART
ANSWERS
TO TOUGH
QUESTIONS

Q: What do you think your legacy will be?

A: I hope it will be that I tried to change the language of business. That I did my best to muster up a revolution in kindness within the business context. That I tried to redefine work as a spiritual endeavour, not just a job, not just a Monday to Friday sort of death. That I just stood up, took it personally and tried to change things.

(Anita Roddick's answer – what's yours?)

And people do live in the past. Everything they think they know is anchored there. Ask someone to tell you about what's going on for them in the present and they'll give you a history lesson. What they saw once, what they felt once, what they heard once, all of it's in the past. Except it's not, of course. All that stuff, which intensifies under the weight of psychological gravity and is called 'Experience', is not in the past, but is now. It shows up now in how people choose to behave, to think, to decide. It shows up in their beliefs, their attitudes and their values. They do what they do now because of what happened to them in the past.

"How do you feel about working for this company Joe?"

"Uh great, I guess."

"And why's that Joe?"

"'Cos they treat you right, I guess."

"What do you mean, they treat you right Joe?"

"Uh. Like they paid my Y2K bonus right on cue. Just like they said they would."

"How about you Becky? How do you feel about working for your company?"

"It's a pile of shite. You wouldn't believe it. It's a joke. I think this lot are having me on sometimes, I really do."

"And Becky, tell me, why do you feel that way?"

"It's the management here. Honestly, what a right laugh, I tell you. Too many chiefs and not enough Indians, that's the problem. It used to be fine here, you know, before the merger. But they've no idea what's going on at my level any more. And they never say thank you, either."

Let's have a Smart look at what's going on here.

Developing [people] still requires a basic quality in the manager which cannot be created by supplying skills or emphasizing the importance of the task. It requires integrity of character.

Peter Drucker

SMART QUOTES

Part of what's going on is that people are natural and unstoppable story-tellers. They make things mean things. Joe gets his $20,000 bonus on time and can buy his little sports car the next day. An event happens. The payment occurs – money is transferred into his account. He makes this mean: "my company is a trustworthy one". The immediate and intense pleasure of driving in his sports car supports and reinforces the meaning he made.

Note that the meaning is in and from Joe and not inherently present in the event itself.

Joe has set up a filter regarding his company, through which he will filter all subsequent events regarding his work life. It will have a huge impact on his ongoing attitude towards his company, maybe towards work in general. It will also create a burden – a weight of expectation – for his company to maintain his filter, to keep his meaning-making accurate. They may or may not be aware of this, nor may they care. If they are not, they'll be missing a great opportunity.

Becky too has set up a filter, though the event which triggered its construction is lost somewhere in the past. It might have been one event, might have been a number of them, but the filter is still there. It's one that tells her that management mistreat people at her company. The filter is so strong that it will likely affect how she views the world. She'll be looking for mistreatment. She'll be expecting to find it. She won't want to be disappointed. Whenever anything occurs which fits her definition of mistreatment, the filter will be reinforced so that she'll be able to tell herself and anyone who is prepared to listen "I told you so." (It's another smart thing to know about people that they like consistency, congruency, alignment. They like to make things fit. But we'll be back to that one later). When things occur that don't fit her filter – like an act of

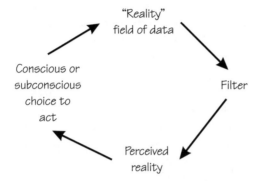

Figure 1.1

management generosity – she is not likely to acknowledge it. She will experience it when it happens, of course, but will not make it mean anything that has the power to override the old meaning. It will just be something that happens.

The filter acts to collect or capture all the things and meaning that prove the filter is correct. Everything else falls through the sieve.

Have a look at Figure 1.1 (a Smart thing to know about people – sometimes they really enjoy a picture or a model). What are the implications of this model?

1. There is more data out there than anyone can possibly process, so our minds are able to attend to only some of it. Some data is ignored; some is passed through into our consciousness unaltered; a lot of that data is modified by passing through the unique filter system we have each acquired over our years of life.

2. Our filter system is mostly unconscious and is triggered automatically when presented with familiar data. The filtering process happens almost instantaneously and we are powerless to stop it.

3. A lot of our filter system, including the most powerfully automatic parts of it, was put there when we were very young – by our parents, by our early childhood experiences, etc. We had no choice about that. It therefore makes no sense at all to beat ourselves up if, for example, we catch ourselves working from our filter system or. Nor does it help to blame anyone else for why they perceive the things they do.

4. Our perceived reality arises out of this filtering process and includes conscious and unconscious thoughts and emotions. Our own unique perceived reality may or may not match closely with "real, objective" reality (whatever that might be). Politicians, for example, thrive on the fact that it is possible to look at the same data and perceive it in vastly different ways (by attaching vastly different meanings to the data)

5. We do have the opportunity to slow down the perception cycle here, to examine our perceived realities, and to ask ourselves questions like:

    "Where did that (thought) (emotion) come from?" or
    "Do I really believe that, or is that just my filter system acting up again?"

    If we don't slow it down by asking these kinds of questions, then we just react automatically and unconsciously out of whatever gets through our filter system. Our filter systems can run our lives without our even being aware of the process.

6. We make decisions and take action our of our examined or unexamined perceived realities, not out of "real reality". Whenever we act, we affect the environment that contains all that data, and thus our own behaviour literally creates the world we live in over time. The employee who believes that his manager "doesn't involve us enough in making decisions" will subtly and unconsciously behave in ways that result over time in him being excluded from the decision-making process. By not participating in meetings, by not asking for information, by not sharing ideas (self-justified because "managers don't listen anyway – they never involve us, you see"), the employee helps create exactly what he most despises.

In this way, all people – managers and managed alike – co-create their organizations. To co-create better and different organizations, we all need to become more competent and proficient at being aware of mental models such as the filter cycle. This is a big challenge to the received wisdom (itself a type of filter) which says that organizations are created by managers and leaders, and inherited by everyone else.

As this book develops, we'll be looking at ways that you can illuminate and challenge the filters that people create to make sense of the (their) world. You'll need to do that for yourself too, since you'll have filters in place that keep you reliving the past. I've met managers who are still trying to recruit their father – or at least someone who reminds them of their father. I've met people who aren't appraising the person in front of them, but someone they managed many years ago.

I've met many many people who can't allow their manager to be the best they can be, because they are determined to make them fit into their conception of how insufficient managers really are. Faced with the future, they continue to live in the past.

And that brings us to one more mental model concerned with the past.

The shadows

If you lead or manage people, you'll need to free them from the past, give them hope for the future and confidence and capability in the present. This book is intended to show you how.

If you lead or manage people, you'll be haunted by the past too – the past of all the managers who ever lived before you, real and fictional. And you'll be haunted by the past that has been created not just by your own behaviours – the promises you've kept and broken have all created a story about you which is being told every day in the hearts and minds of your people – but created by the organization and what's happened there in the past.

And some of what you're haunted by is nothing to do with *you* at all.

KILLER QUESTIONS

What of the past do we want to take with us? And what would we choose to leave behind?

When you become a manager, or reach any position of authority in a company, other people begin to watch you. They can't take their eyes off you. They look at everything you say, everything you don't say; everything you do, everything you don't do. And then they stick a label on that behaviour, they make a meaning out of what you have and haven't done. "He's a joker." "She doesn't care." "He's only looking out for himself."

These meaning-labels are what we all use to make sense of our little worlds: they act like our own personal mythology. Are those meanings "correct"? Are they "fair"? Probably. Not.

But where do the meanings come from? All of them are shaped by the individual character, personal history and psychological make-up (and would that it were as easy to adjust as L'Oréal) of the individual who creates them – but these meanings do share some common origins.

Imagine that this perennial gaze your people shine on you is like a spotlight. What is business but a stage and we but actors in it?

So there you are, playing your part, learning the lines and the moves, trying to do your best, and all the time the spotlight of your colleagues' gaze is following you about.

Occasionally you come upstage and deliver a speech:

   "So, folks, it's change time again . . ."

(You'd probably choose a better opening line than that, but you get my gist).

Well, the thing is, no matter how well you deliver that line, no matter how much you personally believe your message, no matter how scout-camp committed you are to the cause it heralds, your audience aren't looking at you alone.

Because the light they're shining on you is casting shadows.

They're not looking at you alone, nor are they listening to your voice alone. Their attention is distracted – because the shadows their spotlight casts are looming above and behind you.

The first shadow is called the Personal Shadow. It's your shadow side – all the dark parts of your psychological makeup which you'd prefer not to acknowledge and which you mostly do a pretty good job of covering up. That tendency to anger, or sarcasm, or to projecting your weaknesses on to others' behaviours – that's part of your shadow stuff. Most of the time, as I say, you've got it under control. But whenever it slips out, your people will construct a whole new You out of it.

Smart things
to say

> Every day I help create this organization by how I choose to think, talk and act. It is therefore as much my organization as any one's – no matter what level they are at in the company or what their job title is.

The next shadow outwards I call the Shadow of Context. It sounds grand because it is. This shadow holds all the fears people project about the context within in which you are operating. It colours your speech with all the mess of corporate culture and history. So when you say: "Trust me . . ." they don't just hear *you* speak, they hear all the voices of your company's history, real and imagined, who have spoken those words too. So they hear you saying "Trust me" and they remember Mr Tredegar who once asked his department to trust him and then half of them lost their jobs. And when you say "It's OK to make mistakes as long as we learn from them", they remember Jenny in Accounts who once made a mistake and look what happened to her . . . all organizations carry these myths of disablement: they provides a wonderful excuse to stay within the comfort zone. I don't think I've worked with a group who can't remember someone in the company who was "sacked for telling the truth". Chase these stories down, and you'll find that the Man Who Told the Truth in fact took early retirement because of an ingrowing toenail.

The Shadow of Context. They're not listening to you because they're listening to their idea of what the corporate culture says. They're not listening to what you give permission for because they're listening to their idea of what the corporate culture grants. They're not listening to how you're going to break the mould because they're listening to their idea of how the corporate culture has made the mould.

The Shadow of Context is a nightmare for any self-respecting change agent. However much you want to push your people into the future, they want to use what they see hovering behind you as an excuse for dragging you into the past.

But the Shadow of Context is as nothing, nay not even like unto a sharpening of the wind, compared with the next shadow that their probing spotlight inevitably casts behind you. The next shadow is even bigger and more threatening.

The Outer Shadow – the otherwise Unnameable – casts a greater gloom over the work of change agents anywhere in the world. It's not specific to any country or company. The Shadow of Context tells your audience: "Don't trust him, because he, poor schmuck, doesn't understand how this company *really* works . . ." The Outer Shadow tells them: "Don't trust him, because he is *The Boss*."

The Outer Shadow is the one that thrives on every human being's core beliefs about work and organizations. One of those core beliefs is: *Bosses are untrustworthy.*

What a dreadful generalization, yes? But name me more than two characters who are "Bosses" from works of literature, of film, of theatre that are *not* deceitful and malevolent. Our society thrives on images of bosses who do us down, who trick us, who exploit us. From Gradgrind in Dickens to Mr Burns in The Simpsons, in comics and in the movies, bosses are not to be trusted. The boss who tricks us is as deeply held in our consciousness as the English policeman who says "Evenin' all!"

One of the major international courier companies ran a radio advertisement in the UK not so long ago. Its narrator is a secretary who tells us about a competition her boss is running in the company where she works: best money-saving idea wins a lunch – "and he's paying!" she says. After the blurb about how good the courier company is and how much money it really did save the firm, the secretary announces that, to her amazement, she won. Then in the background you hear her being asked "Do you want fries with that?" The punchline, of course, is that her boss has saved himself even more money by taking her for a lunch at McDonald's.

This gag simply does not work unless we unquestioningly accept the premise that bosses do this – they trick you. Bosses exploit. That is part of the deep structure of our society when it comes to work. We may be in the Information Age, but some of your attitudes are still in the Industrial Age.

Shadow 3 is partly created, as all the Shadows are, by the projection of the employee or staff member. If they ever want the Shadows to go away, the first thing they need to do is stop creating the conditions for them – to stop shining the spotlight. You can send a manager on every development course available, and make them fast, flexible, inspirational, clever, a colleague – but if the employee still wants to look for Trickster, Exploiter, The Boss, then things are going to be slow to change.

KILLER QUESTIONS

Where did I get my conceptions about management from? Who am I – consciously or subconsciously – trying to emulate?

One further complication. The Shadows are also sustained, of course, by the behaviour of some bosses – people who step into the role suggested by Shadow 3 and act aloof, bossy, always right, just because they've never been told anything else. Mr Burns influences victor-bosses as well as victim-employees.

And what all that produces is a vicious recycling of old behaviours of the boss–employee relationship:

Me strong, you weak
Me know, you don't know
Me decide, you do . . .

So what can we do about the Shadows?

There ought to be checklist here. Twenty things you can do about the Shadows. But there isn't, because there aren't. In many people, these shadows are so indelible that they'll resist every tactic you try to erase them. If someone is determined to be disempowered, the Shadows they see give them all the evidence they need to stay that way.

However, there are some things to consider . . .

The first tactic might be to share the model with your people – to test its validity in their experience. In other words, use the model to open up a conversation about you, your style, the culture and the nature of power in companies. Tell them you sense these shadows exist, tell them you're not blaming them for seeing them, tell them that you can't really do anything about them. Why? Because ultimately it's they who are creating them with their spotlights, and only they can stop seeing the shadows by focusing on you as a human being rather than a company representative. And that you'd like to answer any questions which might dissipate the shadows.

Then you can look at working through each individual shadow:

Shadow 1 is the simplest to tackle, though that does not make it easy, and certainly not safe. It requires you opening yourself up to feedback that is designed to increase your self-awareness. Insist on upwards or 360 degree appraisals being central to your performance management systems – and be the first to volunteer. (Even then you may find Shadow 3 getting in the way of honest feedback – but you must persevere.)

Smart things
to say

You can anticipate **Shadow 2** resistance by explaining how you are *not* "part of the old culture" and not like "other bosses". But even then, you are at the mercy of your people's capacity for filtering information to suit their needs

Ultimately, here, as in so many aspects of change, acceptance may be the real answer. There's a culture in business which says that everything can be solved, if we had but insight enough and effort. In fact, there are some areas of human existence that are resistant to the easy solution. I believe the Shadows is one of them.

Not all organizational problems can be solved by the actions of organizations alone, no matter how high-minded they might be. **Shadow 3**, the outer shadow, takes us into the realm of the conditioning we all receive from our education and from society concerning what work is for and what we might expect from it. Deleting those old expectations and creating new ones is a personal duty, not an organizational one, and not everyone will see the point of bothering.

The Outer Shadow is sustained by the assumption that people would rather not work and would choose not to if given the half a chance. This is why, still, as the new millennium is born, many companies revolve around rules, policies and procedures that restrict rather than release people. All traditional corporate rules are designed to keep people *in* the company – not just physically, but psychologically and morally, by behaving in a certain way. Even the unwritten rules demand this. I asked one group of managers what Gift they would wish on their employees if they had the chance. (I write the word Gift with a capital G because I suppose I was looking for noble answers such as "regular customer gratitude" or "more time for themselves".) Most of this group, when I'd asked the question, looked at me as if I had a fish on my head. Then one of them said: "I wish they wouldn't win the Lottery; they're all in a syndicate, you see . . ."

Part of the problem here is that most people believe that they are enslaved by their work. Our forefathers have conspired to make work a place of restriction, confinement, effort and exploitation – and until recently we've joined in the conspiracy. We are of a difficult generation – on the cusp of a new world of work where different core beliefs may apply. At the moment however, conditioned by old beliefs, too many people in changing organisations are wandering around, squinting at the day's new light, as if just released from gaol.

KILLER QUESTIONS

Where do our assumptions (about customers, processes, people) come from?

Not all organizational problems can be solved by the actions of organizations alone . . . That's why, though this is a tremendously invigorating time to be working in change, I sometimes wonder if I might add some more value to the world by speaking to some teenagers in school who are just considering their careers.

How many of us, when we start work, get a speech like this from their parents: "Go on, have fun! You'll have a wonderful time! You're about to spend some of the most fascinating, stretching, learning-filled years of your life! I envy you I really

The Modern

1900–1935? ————————————▶ 1935–1970 ————————————▶ Post-modern 1970–2000

Monopoly capitalism Technological determinism Application of scientific method to management Emergence of Fordism Scientific management and the classical school of management	Socio-psychological concerns with alienation and anomie Hawthorne experiments Discovery of group behaviours Research into leadership, moti- vation and job design	Quality management BPR Empowerment Learning organization Corporate governance

Control ————————————————————————————▶ Empowerment

Characterizing features

Bureaucratic structure
Control is external
Separation of ownership and
management
National state regulation
Manufacturing base
Hierarchical knowledge
Constant linear industrial
process through well-defined
stages
Undifferentiated consumers

Characterizing features

Organic structure
Control internalized
Downsizing and teamwork
The global economy
Post-industrial service economy
Information technology
Recognition of limits to progress
creates focus on quality
Differentiated consumers
Industrial relations based on
inner compliance

Depth of organizational development interventions

Shallow (purely technical)

Analysis of functional characteristics, e.g. time and motion
studies

Deep (socio-psychological)

Analysis of individual and team
behaviours

Figure 1.2 Key characteristics of the post-modern organization. Reproduced from Jim Grieves *Navigating Change into the New Millennium: Themes and Issues for the Learning Organisation.*

do . . ." No, that's the speech we get when we go off to university. The speech we get when we launch into our careers is a lot more downbeat ("Get a nice steady job, keep your nose clean, don't upset the boss . . .") – and too few of us ever recover.

Perhaps if we all got a more constructive send off from Mum and Dad, more of us would be more courageous and risk-taking when it comes to living in organizations.

So *there you are* . . .

Not all the problems you're faced with as a manager are your fault. But they are your problem.

And you do have certain responsibilities as a manager.

SMART QUOTES

"Many Dot Coms are about to be exposed for what they are: vapid, shallow, hollow companies."

George Colony
Forrester Research Inc.

Management is the art of choreographing people and resources to achieve the objectives of the organization to a standard of excellence.

What used to be true, in times when change was more sedate and markets and organizations more stable, was that being a manager was a sign that you knew more than your staff. During your years working in and up the company, you had acquired specialist knowledge. Because of this you made all the decisions as a manager, and used the authority of your status to make your employees act on your decisions. You controlled, and you commanded. They did. And people called you Sir. (You, Miss, Mrs or Ms, would probably not be considered for a management position back then.)

Table 1.1

Old Logic	New Logic
Things	Ideas, knowledge
Newtonian	Quantum
Organization as machine	Organization as communities
Hierarchies	Networks
Structure	Process
Action	Interaction
Teaching	Learning
Capital growth	People growth
Information technology	Interaction technology
Market share	Mind share

Source: Goran Carstedt, formerly Head of Retail, Europe at IKEA.

We live and work in turbulent times. Almost every business book released in the last couple of years has featured a list like this – *instant global communication, the impact of IT and telecoms, the relentless explosion of information, the rise of the knowledge economy, escalating competition, unparalleled consumer power, the globalization of markets and economicszthe 'Westernization' of developing countries, increased pressure from shareholders, media and consumers* – and this book is no exception.

These fundamental shifts in the way the world works have brought about a change in the nature and role of management. A new logic is prevailing as context for this new management (see Table 1.1).

And this new logic has brought about some new roles for Smart managers to play.

The new rules (roles) of management

The rules are changing and they are giving birth to new roles for managers. Here are three:

1. Power

Power is not something you have over people; it is what you can demonstrate through people.

Power is defined as the ability to take action. The current business environment demands speedy action.

Old management derived its power from status and politics – from its place in the hierarchy. If you're only level 8 but I'm level 13, you do as I say. Some managers still pull this stunt, of course, but that's because they operate in organizations which cannot bring themselves into the future – and besides, they know that it's easier to live in Shadow 3. These companies may or may not survive, but you, Smart Reader, are unlikely to be in them for long.

> **Smart things to say**
>
> All of us are smarter than any of us

Power in today's management is released through combining the best of everyone's efforts, skills and ideas. That's where the potential for speed comes from – when everyone is focused on the customer and the common purpose rather than whose butt to kiss on the way up the ladder.

2. Synergy

Managers can no longer succeed by themselves. The world of business is so complex that any worthwhile answer to the problems we're facing rarely resides in the genius of one person alone. Smart answers to tough problems are born in the synergistic coupling of everyone's minds. Today's management is about tapping into the knowledge bank that exists within and between people. What we know together may be our only source of competitive advantage.

3. Leadership

People's expectations of work and life have changed fundamentally. People expect to be treated fairly, honestly and to be given the best tools for the job they're asked to do (including information, responsibility and authority). They don't expect to be abused, patronized or neglected. They expect to play a real part in the story of the company. They want to express their talents to the full and expect recognition that they are doing so.

This requires you to play a range of roles within the overall character which is "Manager". At the level of Tasks and activities, you'll need to be an Engineer, designing projects that work and assigning resources accordingly. At the level of Doing, you'll need to be a Teacher, showing people what behaviours are required and how they will help them to do their jobs better by serving the organisational objectives. At the level of Thinking, you'll need to be a Coach, encouraging people to surface their habitual mental models and expanding their capacity for thinking. And finally, at the level of Purpose, you'll need to be a Midwife, helping people give birth to their sense of meaning, their connection to the greater mission of the organization (Figure 1.3).

Figure 1.3

Smart lists

Metaphors and similes for
Old Management

Metaphors and similes for
Today's Management

Schoolteacher	Coach
Policeman	Partner
Watchdog	Counsellor
Ship's captain	Cheerleader
Slavedriver	Gardener
Emperor	Alchemist

Don't try it

If you operate by the old authoritarian, command and control, political power-charged rules you'll suffer, largely because of point 3 above. You're people won't stand for it and you'll be found out.

Unfortunately your company will suffer too, because you'll seriously damage the performance and productivity of the enterprise. You'll impact the performance because the horrible mismatch between command and control bossery and the work values of today's workforce always produces low morale – disaffection, anger and stress. And you'll impact the organization's productivity because you'll suppress the competence and skills of your people. They won't want to share their knowledge with others, and they won't want to turn their capability into exceptional customer service.

After all, why would they? All their energies will be turned towards bitching about you.

So don't try it – give it up. Step with us into the future.

Three management pioneers

Frederick W Taylor (1856–1917), inventor of scientific management, evangelist of measurement, efficiency and control, without much faith in human beings:

> Hardly a competent workman can be found who does not devote a considerable amount of his time to studying just how slowly he can work and still convince his employer that he is going at a good pace.

Elton Mayo (1880–1949), creator of the Hawthorne studies, which called upon managers to realize that human beings in the workplace respond well to recognition, approval and attention and also to being part of a cohesive group.

> So long as commerce specializes in business methods which take no account of human nature and social motives, so long may we expect strikes and sabotage to be the ordinary accompaniment of industry.

Mary Parker Follet (1868–1933), neglected management thinker and humanist:

> I do not think that we have psychological, ethical and economical problems. We have human problems, with psychological, ethical and economical aspects, and as many others as you'd like.

SMART
PEOPLE
TO HAVE
ON YOUR
SIDE

Mary Parker Follett was born in Quincy, Massachusetts in 1868. Most notably a sociologist and a bluestocking social reformer, Mary Parker Follett graduated *summa cum laude* in economics, law, politics and philosophy from Radcliffe College in 1898 and spent the next decade founding several Boston boys' and young men's clubs. This included the Roxbury League, which began the use of schools as community centres.

Like many other women of her class and intellectual achievement, she first went into social work, but unlike many of them, she took what she learned about human relationships and ventured far afield with it.

In her writings and lectures, Follett looked at such things as creative group process, crowd psychology, neighbourhood and occupational associations, alternatives to representative governance, the self in the relation to the whole, and the important ideals of integration, synthesis, and unifying differences. Her focus was on the "community process" of "unifying differences". Follett spent many years writing and lecturing on industrial relations and management. Her advanced theory of management was based on motivation and coordination of group process. She emphasized the importance of relationships in organizations with her writings.

In other words she was not only one of the first humanist management thinkers, she was also one of its first futurists:

> Reading Mary Parker Follett, it is tempting to think there really is nothing new under the sun. Warren Bennis writes that he finds her work, which preceded his own early writings by at least 40 years, "disspiritingly identical" to contemporary leadership theory: she criticised hierarchical organisations and celebrated nonlinearity; she detested competition, bullies and the "command and control" leader-

ship style, favouring instead more "integrated," democratic forms of management. She thought front line employee knowledge should be incorporated into decision-making and suggested to companies that relations with unions might be improved if they tried to understand why a worker might want to make a higher wage or work in better conditions. Like most of her intellectual contemporaries she was in thrall to the new and hugely influential science of psychology, but she never forgot that humans are social creatures linked to other people by means of family and citizenship.

Barbara Presley Noble, reviewing *Mary Parker Follett: Prophet of Management* (HBR Press)

Nevertheless, Mary Parker Follett has never attained the historical stature of some of her contempories. Was this because management science was, in her day, pretty much a men's club? (Her ideas became well known in Japan, the huge distance involved perhaps making her gender an irrelevance.) Certainly she was fated to preach her optimistic ideology of cooperation, negotiation, "constructive conflict" and consensus-making in a world that was either prewar, at war or postwar during much of her professional life. As Peter Drucker points out, politically, the 1930s and 1940s "were dominated by men and creed that knew the proper use of conflict was to conquer".

How to be a better boss

What employees most often accuse their bosses of

There are four things people generally accuse their bosses of. The history of management has produced a wealth of evidence, mostly factual, a lot of it also made up, which now exist in the collective consciousness

A short, Smart history of management

3000 B.C.	Sumerians use written rules for governance
	Egyptians use management practices to build pyramids
2750 B.C.	Babylonians use extensive set of laws and policies for governance
1500 B.C.	Chinese use extensive organization structure for government agencies and the arts
1000 B.C.	Greeks use different governing systems for cities and state
800 B.C.	Romans use organization structure for communication and control
400 B.C.	Socrates discusses management practices and concepts
350 B.C.	Plato describes job specialization
A.D. 500	Venetians use organization design and planning concepts to control the seas
A.D. 900	Alfarbi lists traits of effective leaders

Source: R.W. Griffin, *Management* (1996).

of all employees that "proves" managers aren't worthy of respect. It's in their Shadows around bosses in general, and specifically in the Shadows they project around you.

If you can respond well to these four challenges, you'll be well on the way to success. Here they are:

1. S/he doesn't appreciate the work I do.

2. S/he's not in touch with the day to day work I do.

3. S/he's one of "them" now, only interested in strategy and the big picture.

4. S/he never tells me what's going on.

And before we go any further with this book, let's tackle what you can do about these four complaints. Remember, they may not be your fault, but they are your problem.

1. S/he doesn't appreciate the work I do.

> Say "Thank You" for work completed, for effort made, for energy expended. Better still, say it as if you mean it. In order to carry that off, you'll need actually to understand what the person did that was worthy of appreciation. See point 2.

Smart rule of thumb

2. S/he's not in touch with the day to day work I do.

> Demonstrate interest in your people's work in your deeds as well as your words. Every day take time – 15–20 minutes – to have a conversation with one of your team. Don't just ask "How's it going?" Say "Show me how it's going."

Smart rule of thumb

3. S/he's one of "them" now, only interested in strategy and the big picture.

> From their perspective, your work is a mystery. So help people understand the work you do and the conflicting demands on your time. When you do talk about the big picture, connect your individual team members' activities to it. Teach people how an organization works, how complex it is.

Smart rule of thumb

4. S/he never tells me what's going on.

Smart rule of thumb

Tell people what's going on. And check that what you're saying is really what they want to know. In team meetings, ask: "What would you most like to hear about?"

KILLER QUESTIONS

How can we get our people to care about our customers if our people don't feel we care about them?

How to be better bossed

What to do when your own boss is the problem

Most of this book, and many like them, send loads of advice your way about becoming a great person to be managed by. What is often overlooked is the *quis custodes* angle. Every boss has a boss – even the CEO answers to the Chairperson, the Chairperson to the stakeholders etc. – so what do you do when you find yourself tempted to join the common gripe that says "we all hate the boss"?

Here are six pieces of advice:

1. *Attempt to understand your boss better.* Good questions to ask are: what are his or her goals – what are his or her business results (the things they are trying to do for the company) and what are their personal wins (the things they are trying to do for their ego or ambition)? What are you doing to satisfy both?

Richard Branson

There are few businessmen who have been as flamboyant – or as successful – as British tycoon Richard Branson. He is the founder of the Virgin Music label, Virgin Atlantic Airways, Virgin Cola, Virgin Brides (complete with that photo . . .), and, more recently, the much-maligned Virgin Trains. Branson is a peerless self-publicist, keeping himself in the public eye and with it his brand. His espoused business principles are to do with people focus (his order of priority is: people, then customers, then shareholders) and agility (when his companies become too big, he tries to reduce them in size). His strategy has always been to be an iconoclast, challenging the big boys (BA, Coca-Cola) whenever he can. But what makes Branson such an attactive proposition is that he knows how to enjoy himself. The chances are that no one has had as much fun on the road to becoming a billionaire as Richard Branson has done.

2. *Understand especially your boss's motivators and measures for success* – what most satisfies him or her and what has to happen for that satisfaction to occur?

3. *Don't generalize* – you say your boss "doesn't seem to care". But what specifically is the behaviour you see which makes you interpret it as "not caring". What would your boss need specifically to do to demonstrate "caring"?

4. *Pick your battles* – you have your hands full making yourself into a better boss for your team, and through that work, making yourself a better human being. Are you really sure you have the time, energy to change your boss?

5. *Learn from it*. Every great boss is an inspiration, a walking vision of what management could be. Every bad boss you have is like a walking training video called "How not to do it!"

6. *Clarify* what you can gain from this position (your own personal wins and business results) and if those things are not sufficiently compelling, plan your exit strategy

Q: How can I make sure that my boss and I are both looking for the same results? How can I makes sure we have a good "psychological contract" for working together?

A: First, list the key wants you have of your boss. Then ask your boss to make a list of key wants he or she has of you. After you have both completed your lists, exchange lists and then meet together to see whether you can agree on a contract that represents a reasonable balance between what your group or department requires to meet its commitments to the overall organisation and what you need . . .

(Adapted from Peter Block, Flawless Consulting)

Q: And then I could do the same for each of my employees . . . ?

A: That's correct, you could . . .

Is your career on the fast track?

This book will help you be a manager of sensitivity and power. But where will you take your career? Here are two questions to consider if you want to become a high flyer:

1. Do I know what I offer and what value I add?

Success may be elusive if you expect it to happen just because you think you're wonderful. Your wonderfulness needs to be translated into value to others: if you weren't around, what would the world/the organization be missing? What are you in the world? A problem solver? [If so, prove it . . .] A problem identifier? [If so, prove it . . .] A community builder [If so, . . .]? A project deliverer? [If . . .] A persuader? [. . .] What are you that is worthy of "success"? And can you prove it in action?

SMART QUOTES

> Never continue in a job you don't enjoy. If you're happy in what you're doing, you'll like yourself, you'll have inner peace. And if you have that, along with physical health, you will have had more success than you could possibly have imagined.
>
> Rodan of Alexandria

2. In what ways am I front of mind?

Imagine if an employee of yours asked for an informal performance appraisal next week? What would it demonstrate? Their eagerness to learn, certainly. Their keenness to understand how they are doing in relation to their ambitions, definitely. And they would assure you that they were courageous – asking for feedback is one of those things that intellectually we all see the value of but emotionally can be a bit of a challenge to say the least. And there's more. Asking for feedback forces *you* to *think* – to reflect on the qualities, characteristics and potential of the person who is asking for the feedback. In other words, asking for feedback from others makes them play an advert of you in their head – without you having to be pushy or arrogant.

Asking for feedback puts you front of mind. So be someone who's not afraid of asking for feedback.

Two other associated points:

- Asking for help shows you're strong enough to consider overcoming your limitations.

- Offering help shows you're confidant enough to transcend your selfishness and create something better with others.

Can you give compelling answers to these two questions? Great. You're destined for the fast track.

But, in the meantime, you need to become a great manager.

Let's get to work!

God

All knowing, all seeing, everywhere, beyond time, creator of everything, but not responsible for your management skills, nor for the painful slowness of the web when America wakes up.

2

Choices

> **A Smart Thing to Know about People**
>
> Life is a product of choices; people are choosing between alternatives every day.
>
> So why would anyone choose you?

In this chapter we will examine your role in managing the "most valuable resource" in your company: talent. How can you attract and retain the best people?

If I had been writing this book ten years ago, the management landscape would have looked pretty different – and so, consequently, would the managerial toolkit.

The obsessions of the late 1980s were externally focused – the market position of the company appeared to be vital above all other considerations and techniques for maintaining the relative health of the organization included benchmarking, downsizing and cutting costs. The budgetary planning process emphasized the short term.

Business writers and thinkers of today look back on those approaches not so much as "wrong" but as only "right" for their time. A more stable business environment allowed pretty accurate analysis of the external environment, with the intention that what you learnt when you looked out into the world would be valuable and implementable as a strategy (that is when you'd got sufficient important people together to have a go at writing the strategy . . .).

Now the world is moving so much faster and so unpredictably (all together now with the mantra: "Paradox, Chaos, Complexity", "Paradox, Chaos, Complexity", "Paradox, Chaos, Complexity",) that the focus has shifted to the internal environment of organizations – and how that impacts our interactions with the world and our customers. So, for example, leaders emphasize growth rather than costs, intellectual capital rather than market position, and a longer-term perspective perceiving the company as a living organism which could, conceivably, live forever rather than a machine which could break down at any time unless we keep tinkering with it. The external focus is still there, of course, and relationship with the customer is more intimate and interactive than ever before, it is what we in the organization need to do to satisfy the customer that matters.

Some approaches widely respected only a few short years ago are now struggling for legitimacy. Copying the perceived "best practice" of competitors, for example, has been almost universally seen as a flawed approach for two main reasons. Firstly, it is incorrect to assume that your company shares the same attributes, assets and culture as mine

Chris Agyris

Chris Agyyris has been James Bryant Conant Professor of Education and Organizational Behaviour since 1971. A prodigious intellect and writer, Agyris has devoted himself more than many in the management field to the complexities and frustrations of human nature. He is most renowned for the concepts of single loop learning – where organizations discover and correct problems without any change to norms, policies and values of the company – and double loop learning – where organizations detect and correct errors by challenging and modifying the underlying norms, policies and objectives. His message that those who are unwilling to let go of their personal agendas are those who will also fail to learn – and therefore damage the capacity of their companies to survive – has influenced heavily Peter Senge's work on learning organizations.

(and that I therefore can easily apply what I learn about what you do well). Secondly, the process of carrying out a major benchmarking project is so involved and time-consuming that by the time it is completed, I may well find that I have armed myself with a wealth of information about you which is no longer applicable to my own necessarily changed position.

Today the perspective is truly inward-looking – seeking to learn about what happens within the organization and how that might impact performance (e.g. corporate culture), and even what goes on within the hearts and minds of employees. Intellectual capital theories discuss the value of intangibles such as knowledge and creativity in terms of competitive advantage. So widespread is this emphasis, so complete the shift in perspective from external to internal in the last decade, that you would be hard pressed to find a major organization that did not describe its human resources as its most "valuable assets".

What this all means to the Smart manager

The role of the manager up until very recently was to play his or her part in the implementation of a strategy formulated at the top of the organization by senior directors who had long experience in the market-place, and thus had learned what worked and what didn't. Your job was to carry out the tasks which your area was responsible for and ensure that your staff conformed to project deadlines, worked within strict budgetary constraints (i.e. kept costs as low as possible), achieved an appropriate quality of work and maintained a sense of discipline and professional conduct.

In some ways, your job hasn't changed at all. You'll be in trouble if you pay a bunch of drunkards and wasters to run up enormous costs and deliver late (apologies if this sounds all too familiar in your company!). So you as a manager have got to keep things focused on quality and customer satisfaction.

SMART QUOTES

> Take away my people, but leave my factories, and soon grass will grow on the factory floors. Take away my factories, but leave my people, and soon we will have a new and better factory.
>
> Andrew Carnegie

But now there is so much more to your job. Now you are responsible not just for Tom, Dick and Harriet, but the the training, experience, judgement, intelligence, relationships and creativity that these individual employees hold in their heads. That is the human capital of your organization, and because it can't be copied by anyone else (they may not look it, but Tom, Dick and Harriet are unique) it may well be true to say that it is the one true potential source for sustained competitive advantage. The essence of success is not your company's products and services (because they can be copied and, if they are any good, they probably will be) but the dynamics of its behaviour and its unique capabilities – its ability to generate knowledge, connect. What you need to be now as a manager is someone who can get the best out of your people so that they can combine with others to keep making products or services better. You need to continuously develop your employees, keep the innovation high and ensure that everyone can continuously adapt to change. For the moment, no one else has got your people's knowledge and competencies, and it is your job to ensure that they are ready and willing to pass it on to you for the greater good of the whole. Tom, Dick and Harriet are suddenly very important. That marks a profound shift from the previous generation of managers who were taught to view human resources as costs.

KILLER
QUESTIONS

Some of this last generation may have managed you and added to your own Shadow (see Chapter 1) about what managers should be like with people. Beware. Ask:

- Which managers am I trying to copy, consciously or subconsciously?
- What assumptions underlie my management style and approach?
- Where did I learn about being a manager?

But isn't Human Resources supposed to be managing people?

Ah, good challenge! But sadly, the answer is no. The profound and remarkable shift from people as costs to people as primary assets has been confused by the actions of companies over the last decade – and how they have utilized HR:

People management abounds with paradoxes. In the prevalent climate, managements tell employees how important they are and how empowered the organization wishes them to be. In the past decade of cost cutting and repeated restructuring, however, employees have learnt to hear that they are the firm's most valuable assets but to understand they are also the most expendable assets. It is ironic for HR specialists that in a period when business strategy has turned to resource based theories of the firm as the dominant paradigm in current strategic analysis, the legacy of the 1980s policies poses huge problems in terms of employee response. The Price Waterhouse Change Integration Team (1996), describe two paradoxes in HRM. Paradox 1 is that at a time of continual down-sizing as a management approach, the human resource is being recognized more widely than ever before as a key to organization success. Paradox 2 is that as the importance of people is increasingly recognized by corporate strategists and managers, where is the HR department?

Pam Swain, "The Learning Organization." *Organizational Learning*, Vol. 6(1), 1999, 30–37

Where is the HR department? Probably in the psychiatrist's office, after the last decade. Think about it. They'd only just got themselves a new name – HR used to be called the Personnel Department – when their reputations as the people people was shattered by the necessity of having to carry out literally millions of exit interviews worldwide in the name of downsizing, and overseeing the administration of an equal number of redundancy payments or early retirement packages. Not so much getting the best out of the people as getting them out of the door.

The last decade had a seriously negative impact on perceptions of HR as a major force in an organization's destiny. In an international study carried out in 1996, T.P. Flannery and others from The Hay Group reported that non-HR managers saw HR not only as a non-player in the change process, but frequently as an impediment to effective organizational change, as they had no understanding of strategic management issues. Pam Swain goes on to draw some inevitable conclusions from Flannery's research:

> This finding was validated by a separate study by Hay McBer in which a survey of 1,500 HR professionals found few who took a strategic perspective or even understood basic strategic change strategies such as re-engineering. If an organization was really serious about creating a more dynamic culture and, for example, changes in approaches to compensation were decided upon, then an initial step was to remove the focus of any changes in people management away from the HR department.

Oo-er!

So as a manager you have to do the quality, cost and customer satisfaction basics but also you need to provide a healthy and compelling place to work. People probably may not trust the HR Department – but they just might trust you.

What would "a healthy and compelling place to work" look like? That's the province of the next chapter. In the meantime, let's assume you have a healthy workplace to offer. In it you have accepted your role as manager and HR executive combined, and you've accepted that because you know people are key to your organization's success (and your own, for that matter).

Smart things to say

I am the human resources department. I am responsible for bringing the best out of this organization's human resources

But first things first. How do you attract and retain the best people available?

Recruiting the best people: healthy hiring practices

It used to be that the scarcest commodity in business was stuff like oil or coal. Competitive advantage came from being the company who could get nearest to the black stuff first.

Then the scarcest commodity for a time was customers – could your company get a powerful market share?

At the start of the e-commerce age, the scarcest commodity was finance – could you persuade the venture capitalists that their money was more wisely invested in your start-up than in the one down the road?

Now the scarcest commodity is people. Not just any people, but the right people – the right stuff.

The new economy companies can't recruit talented people fast enough and the consequent "talent shortage" is the biggest obstacle they face to the ambitious growth targets they've set becoming a reality (Netscape went from two to 2000 employees in its first three years).

And finding a way to overcome this obstacle is their greatest priority.

Your company may or may not feel that it is a "new economy" organization, but whether you're producing widgets, software or cheese, as a manager you'll be responsible for bringing the most competent available people into your organization. Your product or service – and your day-to-day sanity – is only as healthy as the people on your team.

And it won't just be a question of whether the new people you find have the right skills or technical know-how; you'll need to be sure that they have the right attitudes and characteristics to fit into your current team and the wider organizational culture.

SMART QUOTES

"One machine can do the work of fifty ordinary men. No machine can do the work of one extraordinary man."

Elbert Hubbard

So what's the secret to hiring the best people into your organization? And once you've got them, what can you do to make sure they stay with you?

There are four distinct elements involved in bringing people into your organization:

1. *Recruitment* – here you need to know how about the new rules of attraction; where to look for talent and how can you make your place known to all those talented people out there.

2. *Selection* – here you need to know that talented people will be making a choice, between you and possibly many other companies – so there's an art to making their choice easier. And you'll need to know how to choose between alternative candidates

3. *Induction* – here you need to know that first impressions count, and that there are things you can do to make those all so important first days and weeks a confirmatory experience, rather than a regretful one.

4. *Management* – here you need to practice those retention skills which encourage people to choose to stay in your company

Here are some key pieces of advice:

1. Get everyone involved.

Recruitment may serve the strategic aims of the company, but that is no reason for it to be left to a few senior decision-makers. Get everyone involved.

Your people can be your very best recruitment consultants. They are certainly best PR merchants. Do you think that young Samantha is a quiet, shy type, whose only interest seems to be doing the job of writing code? You should hear the fluency and imagination with which she describes working in your company when she's together with her mates at the end of the working day . . .

You'd also be a fool to underestimate the size of Samantha's circle of influence. Even in her relatively short career, she'll have built up a network of contacts – as will Jim, Bob and Tina who sit in that side of the office. Add all those networks together, and you have a fast-moving channel for good and bad gossip about your company – and of course a powerful way of searching out the next new recruit.

SMART
ANSWERS
TO TOUGH
QUESTIONS

Q: What shall we put in our recruitment ads?

A: Relevant and distinct recruitment advertising should be less about telling potential employees what they want to hear and more about revealing the true nature, vision, personality of an organization.

Many companies pay bonuses to those people who are responsible for introducing a talented new hire into the organization.

2. Become a talent magnet

Publicize your company as a great place to work in places that you know potential candidates will be frequenting. Can you get a banner on the cooler websites? Can you sponsor the quiz night at the local wine bar/sports bar? How can your organization have a presence – both for listening for talent and pushing itself as an attractive employer – at relevant conferences, universities, chat rooms?

3. Know what you are looking for

How can you find these special people if you don't know what you're looking for? What technical and attitudinal traits are necessary for the post you're trying to fill? Draw up a list. Which of these are must-haves and which nice-to-haves? Don't compromise.

4. Keep a database of people you know are talented

Use your team's network to this effect. Update it with recommendations from your new hires. Ask them: "Who would you bring in to our company from your old company and why?" Talented people tend to know other talented people.

5. Don't forget you're not just hiring the candidate

. . . You're recruiting his or her family too. Enquire about

Smart things
to say

Talent makes capital
dance

Smart things
to say

Recruiting and retaining talent is all our
business and we should be working
at it all the time

them. If the candidate is new to the city you're in, do you need to do a selling job on the area? Do you need to provide information and support so that people can get settled quickly (education, council, leisure information?) Is there anything you can do to help the family feel good about this person joining your company. After all, you will be the reason this new employee hardly sees their loved ones from now on. Why not send them a card at least to say hello?

SMART QUOTES

> Traditionally, companies get serious about hiring when they have a specific opening: "Our vice president of marketing quit, so we need a new one," or "We want to enter the market for a new kind of computer chip, so we need a team of designers." I call that approach "coincidence hiring": "I happen to need a basketball player today. Did Michael Jordan happen to quit his job?" The odds that he did are not very good. So what are the odds of your landing him? The companies I work with – Cisco, HP, Microsoft, Nike, Schwab – don't want to hire unemployed people or unhappy people. They want to hire people who can make a difference, the best of the best. But those people usually have a good job and are happy where they are. So recruiting them requires a different mind-set. You have to go from coincidence hiring to continuous hiring.
>
> Professor John Sullivan, Head of the human-resource management program at San Francisco State University

The hiring interview

What most people have in their head when it comes to thinking about a hiring interview is some gruelling, torturous interrogation held by stern representatives of the organization. They usually play the role of gate-keepers, or bouncer ("You can't come in here, mate"). The power is definitely and explicitly with the interviewer, and the interviewee is treated as some poor pup who has to justify why he or she should ever think themselves worthy of even applying for a job in the Holy Temple. In what ways can they possibly be good enough?

When people have things like that in their heads (both interviewer and interviewee), it is bound to shape the behaviour of the participants, one defensive, cold, aloof, the other nervous, desperate to please.

I'd like to give you some other mental images about the hiring interview, in the hopes that it produces a different experience, more pleasurable and learningful for both sides.

There's a passive and an active role you need to play.

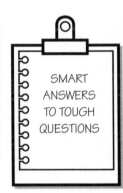

Q: Why can't HR do the interviewing?

A: Because only you have the feel you do for the needs and requirements of the post you're trying to fill and its impact on the rest of the team. And as a manager you need to keep current about what's going on in the outside world. Organizations can be closeting and inward-looking places. Hiring interviews are a great way for you to keep learning about what real people are thinking about your industry and your company.

SMART
ANSWERS
TO TOUGH
QUESTIONS

Passive – your job is to listen

Give the candidate every opportunity to talk.
It's their interview, not yours.

Let there be silence.
Allow them to give considered responses, rather than pat, rehearsed answers that they prepared in advance. Ask questions that demand consideration – and respect the person enough to give them the space to reflect.

Listen for what's said
Yes, you need to hear about their responsibilities to date, their experience and their technical skills; bit listen also for what they tell you about what they value, what their aspirations are, what they love, what they hate . . .

Listen for what's not said
What "meaning" are you assigning to this person? What impression are you building up of their communication skills, honesty, sense of humour, imaginative capability and self-esteem. Are you connecting with this person? Would they connect with your team?

Listen for connection rather than just looking for "fit"
If you sense that this person is really going to enhance your organization or team, then you should get them into it and then find them the job that best fits their talents and your needs. Only looking for someone to fill the hole left by the previous person's departure narrows your search to the job attributes rather than the human potential.

Why are they here?
What was the activating event that made them either leave or consider leaving their last or current job? What does that tell you about their values?

Ask questions that unlock true motivation and values (drivers of talent). For example

- Why are you on this career path? Why choose this line of work out of all other possibilities?

- What do you want to be doing two jobs from now?

- What stories you can tell show how you demonstrate performance under pressure?

- Tell me about a time when you laughed at yourself.

Active – your turn to talk

Be a storyteller.

Stories convey meaning, not just facts.

Traditionally, managers think people want (a) a job, and (b) the money that comes with a job. And of course people do want these things, but they are low-level, basic needs. Once they know that they can satisfy those needs, people will move on to what really they are looking for . . . and they'll need to (literally) hear that you can do that.

My advice is to prepare in advance of the interview a number of true stories that would convince the candidate that when they work for you they will:

- be respected as a human being;

- be communicated with regularly and effectively;

- be listened to;

- be given acknowledgement and recognition;

- be able to do work that makes a difference to the company.

If the candidate is at all Smart, they'll also be asking you to tell stories that convince them that your corporate values are in alignment with your practices. So when you describe what it's like working for your organization, they'll be listening for whether you talk about service or politics, product quality or revenue generation.

All of these things are more meaningful and therefore attractive to the candidate than any list of benefits such as luncheon vouchers or dress-down Fridays that you'll be able to recite.

Be aware too that candidates will be assessing your organization in the reception area as much as in the interview room. What can you do to ensure that first impressions count? Can you enrol the receptionist or the security guard into being a Welcoming Host rather than a Guardian of the Signing-In Book?

Smart things to do

What if you hear about a particular person that you know you want, even though you also know that they are quite happy in their current post? Answer: operate a KIT (Keep In Touch) policy. Millions of sales people do this to remain in the mind of lukewarm prospects or past customers, so that when the opportunity to sell them again, the sales person won't be a stranger. Why not apply this to your recruitment policy?

- Send your target person newsletters or other corporate updates.

- Invite them to speak as your guest at in-house conferences.

- Send them articles written by experts employed by your company, or interviews with the CEO.

- Invite them to work-related socials activities or informal team build events.

- Ask them if they'd ever be interested in working on small projects, perhaps just doing a day or two during their next vacation as a strategic consultant.

- Keep current on any career developments they make – promotions, new responsibilities – and send congratulations accordingly.

- Do they have a personal web page? Sign the guest list.

Hitting the ground running: the induction process

Let's assume now that your skills as a recruiter has brought you success. You made the offer and they said "Yes!" Now what?

There are no excuses for making a new hire feel like a stranger. Any human being in a new role – no matter what level in the organization – is going to have some feelings of trepidation and nervousness.

They will also be operating like a human being and making things mean things. Nothing that happens to them on that first day will be without meaning. If they turn up in the lobby and the receptionist doesn't know who they are or where they should be sent, that will mean something (big) to the newcomer.

So be there to welcome them with a human touch. Then make sure that there's someone with a personality and credibility (otherwise ask HR to help) who will help answer every one of a new recruit's questions:

- How do I work the desktop?

- Who's who around here?

- What's the culture of this place? What are the written and unwritten rules that get things done?

- What work is going on in my area?

- What am I going to do first and how does that fit in to the bigger picture?

- Who are my team mates and what do I have to bear in mind about each of them?

- What's the purpose and strategy of this organization?

- What's the recent history and achievements of this organization?

- Where do I hang my coat?

Someone will also need to ensure that the legal, domestic, personnel, admin and safety issues are also covered.

There are also no excuses for making a new hire feel like a spare part. It takes planning and time to make sure that every new recruit has a desk and the requisite technology (like a computer and an email address).

But inducting a new person into an organization is not just about that individual – it's about the people they'll be working with.

There are absolutely no excuses for not letting a team know that a new hire is coming in next week, so that they can prepare to make that person feel at home, and get over their natural shyness/aggression towards strangers. Whether its your job or HR's, make sure that the team in question knows

- who is coming in – name, background, favourite colour, etc.;

- why they've been recruited – what skills and capabilities they have;

- why they've been recruited – again – why it was necessary for the company to bring someone in;

- how they'll fit in – what work they'll be doing and who they'll be working with on day 1;

- what all this means to the existing team.

Two good ideas for the induction process

Assign a buddy

Someone who will hold the new recruit's hand during the first difficult weeks in their new job. An established team member who can be the source of information about everything from how to get the best out of the IT Helpdesk to what the MD really does have in the boot of her car . . .

Hold a quiz

When I went to St Edmund Hall in Oxford, the tutor Bruce Mitchell, bless him, used to have a way of getting new students familiar with the Bodleian Library, a labyrinthian place with hardly the most up-to-date and user-friendly "customer interfaces". Rather than ask students to go and simply look at the library, or to read the Introductory Manual to try and learn how it worked, he gave us a list of books – or rather details about certain books – which we would have to locate in the library. There was no way we could find out these details *unless we taught ourselves* how to use the library.

Why not build on Bruce's idea? Set new hires a list of questions, about everything from business processes to product specification, from customer profiles to how the bonus scheme works. Design it so that the only way they can get the answers is if they force themselves to go out into the organization, meet some people and do some research and learning. The point behind this being not that they prove if they are clever or compliant, but that they learn valuable information whilst doing something even more important: extending their network and laying the foundations of a sense of community.

At the other end of the relationship

The exit interview

Life tells us to expect and even welcome change through embracing that which is new. Sometimes the change you need to embrace is the fact that one of your people – maybe one you worked particularly hard to get into your company – wants to say goodbye.

Smart managers extract maximum benefit from a person leaving the organization. If you've got a staff turnover rate way above the industry average, you need to know why. Even if not, a departing employee could give you some invaluable feedback on the corporate culture in general and your managerial effectiveness in particular.

Exit interviews are powerful sources of learning for organizations, but one rarely used to full effect. That's because if someone has decided to move on to another job, there will be some negative feelings about your company lurking somewhere in their decision-making process. And those negative feelings might be about you. Apparently the top reason most people leave their job is not because the money or opportunity was better elsewhere, but because they didn't like their boss.

Now some of the feedback you and the company get in an exit interview may be quite emotional, since the leaver is still very close to the turmoil of the decision. You have two choices here:

- You can decide to take everything that is said and with honest reflection and high integrity, listen through the emotion to the "truths" that you need to hear.

- You can decide to hold a post-exit interview, held say three months after the leaver is in their new post. Distance might lend a measure of objectivity to the feedback.

What you must never do is dismiss the learning and feedback that your intuition tells you you really need to hear, but which your ego tells you is simply the gripes of a disgruntled ex-employee. And what you must never do is avoid having an exit interview because you're scared of what you might hear. I've known managers go out of their way to explain how the ex-employee "really didn't want to have an exit interview, you know', when what they really mean was that *they* didn't want to hold one.

One final point on exit interviews. When someone leaves you, it's an expression of their personal choice. It is not a personal affront to you and your inability to build loyalty and commitment (unless it really, really feels like that to your intuition, in which case this person's exit is another step on your never-ending learning curve).

Extending the relationship beyond your company

And maybe there isn't a lot of negative, emotional feedback that you're going to hear. Talented people move on for many reasons – for reasons of growth and experimentation, or because they've had a personal crisis (like a divorce or a 30th or 40th birthday). They might just be moving house. For whatever reason, people move on.

But that's not a reason to consider the relationship as over, particularly if we are talking about a really talented employee. Keeping in touch with them might keep the door open for them to return at some point. Even if that's not going to be possible, maintaining a relationship with them after you've stopped paying them is a great way of keeping your ear to the ground in industry developments. Ex-employees can also be great ambassadors for your company.

Why not:

Smart things
to say

We get the talent
we deserve

- Send them the company or team newsletter?

- Invite them to corporate social events:

- Invite them to participate in corporate-sponsored conferences?

- Just call them up to say "hi" from time to time?

Retention: holding on to the best

> [The goal] is to keep people so busy having fun everyday that they don't even listen when the headhunters call.
>
> Ken Alvares

The very things that make your company attractive to a candidate who is considering joining you are the same things that could retain an employee who is considering leaving you. People are looking for some or all of these elements of a "good job':

- long-term career paths;

- very specific technical/project experience;

- training and development;

- fair and flexible compensation packages;

- bonuses and benefits (car, health insurance, etc.);

- up-to-date and performance-enhancing work environment and infrastructure (= a decent chair and sufficient computer memory).

And then some of the softer, but equally compelling, things.

- Challenging and stretching goals (both personal and corporate). Why? Because people seek meaning. They want to connect to something of purpose. What compelling purpose does your team/company have?

- Strong interpersonal relationships with peers

SMART
PURPOSE
EXERCISE
IN FIVE
MINUTES

He who has a why to live for can bear almost any how. (Nietzsche)

Human beings make things mean things, and if they don't find meaning, they'll create one (even if it's "this is meaningless" or "it's a crap meaning"). Human beings search for meaning.

It may also be said that human beings are in search of meanings which are inspirational, life-affirming, purposeful, altruistic, creative, for the greater good. This is the spiritual dimension of all human endeavour.

Once people have worked out that money alone doesn't buy you happiness, they generally look for work which is meaningful, or join together with others for some common purpose.

Purpose exists behind the veil of the banal. That's why your job is not to be satisfied with the obvious suggestion that: "we just write code, mate". True, but to what end? In what spirit do you just write code mate?

This sense of common purpose and focus is what organizations have been trying to access with their missions, visions and value statements.

The trouble is, purpose and meaning is something, like love, which suffers from being reduced to words. the heat and passion that fuels the visionary often dies when the wordsmiths get their pens out.

That does not, however, diminish the energy-releasing capacity of purpose.

Try discussing these questions with your team:

1. Beyond the obvious mechanical realities of making profit and pleasing customers, why do we exist?

2. We are here to enable . . . customers to . . . colleagues to . . . shareholders to . . . society to . . .

3. When they write the words on our tombstone, what will they say?

4. If we weren't here, what would this organization lose?

5. What's unique, special or valuable about this team/group/company?

6. What are we proud of?

7. What would we like to tell our children about how we went about our lives at work?

8. What object, image or metaphor best symbolizes our purpose?

Why? Because people are social. Work is a place where people test their capacity for connection. People are attracted to other people. Other people are (can be) where the fun is in work – and certainly where the stretch and challenge is. It is certainly where loyalty exists in the 21st century. People will report that they like working with their team mates when they have little knowledge or respect for the aims of the company. Even in a project-based organization, where people can be working together for relatively short periods of time, the socialization pull is strong (or should be if you as a manager give it time and resource).

- Trust, acknowledgement, respect *for* management.
  Why? Because people have in their collective consciousness a huge data bank of personal and inherited material which tells them to distrust management. Another instinct in them tells them that being led well can be an inspirational experience, so they continue to look for it.

- Trust, acknowledgement, respect *from* management.
  Why? Because people want to be of value and be valued. They want to hear "thank you". Whether this instinct comes from their altruism or their core insecurity, nevertheless recognition of effort tells them that they, somehow, somewhere and at least once in their fleeting lives made a difference in the world. (Hint: don't make recognition a once-in-a-lifetime event!)

- Autonomous job design.
  Why? Because we are living in a customized world. Click on at Amazon.com and it greets you with your name. Most search engines or hub sites allow you to personalize their layout, so that you get the bits that you particularly want first. If you can have myexcite.com, why not myworkexperience.org? Give someone a part-time contract – if it really suits their personal domestic arrangements. Give another access

to projects over which they feel they have overarching influence – if it suits their ambitions? Give another reimbursement for a particular training course (one that's not on your organization's standard and HR-approved roster) if you know it would really bring benefit to both a particular staff member and the company.

These, then, are the ways that you can make a personal difference to retaining talent in your organization.

However, there are some ifs and a but.

The ifs are these. The job elements we've listed here only remain seductive:

- *If* they are refreshed and enhanced by the organization over time, so that they remain relevant to the demands and desires of the present day. What people need and expect from their working lives changes over time

- *If* they are, as far as possible (and even farther if you're trying to make a big impression on a particularly valuable employee), tailored to the individual needs and status of the employee

- *If* they grow out of a genuine respect by the company for the requirements and concerns of people, rather than cynically being used only as negotiating cards when the heat is on.

And the but?

There's no but. I was just saying that to keep you reading.

No, I'm kidding. There is a big but.

The reality of the situation is that what actually keeps people in your company is their personal choice – something that they reappraise, consciously or subconsciously, every day. You can create things that stop people looking for the exit signs in your company, but you can't stop the pull of personal ambition within a life-frame.

Nor can you stop the pull of the market place. For every effort you make to make your organization the "place to be", your competitors are doing the same things, increasing the stakes (and they're buying out stock options and offering big signing-on bonuses).

The only way to stop this feeling like an ugly power play is to change the way you think and feel about employing people.

> Perhaps employers should think less about building fences to keep people in and think more about how they can be magnets where people stay because they respect the companies they work for and love their jobs.
>
> Simon Howard, *The Sunday Times*, 1 October 2000

Your staff are not corporate slaves, shackled to your company out of a desperate fear that next month they won't be able to pay the mortgage.

Nor are they battle-scarred mercenaries, holding you to ransom with their talent and intellectual capital.

They are people, human beings who are making a choice, based on their values and principles and hopes and ambitions. They hope, by working for you, to express something of those values and move closer to their ambitions.

KILLER QUESTIONS

Why do we work (here)?

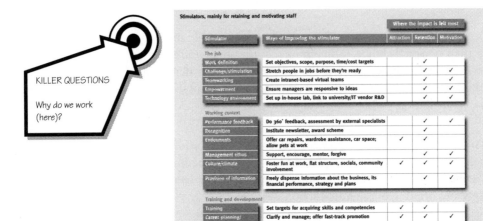

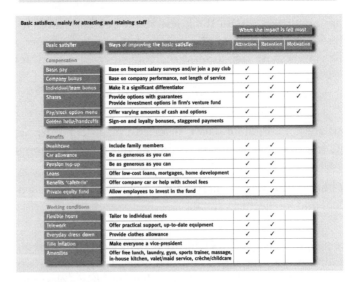

Figure 2.1 Reproduced with permission from Evolving Competencies for IS Lite by Gartner Executive Programs (www.gartner.com)

Do we need to retain everyone?

Do we know which activities are key and need high levels of (valuable) competence? Which activities are most valued in the marketplace? Which posts are relatively easy to fill?

Do we need to retain everyone for ever?

There will be some staff who you think are key who are in fact only key for the length of a particular project (year 2000 was a major, worldwide example of this). This may be an argument for making as much work as possible project-based . . .

What is Plan B when our most valued employees leave?

Do what you fear the most: consider what to do when Mission-Critical Margaret ups and leaves. You, the project, the company will survive, but it'll be easier if you think about it now rather than when you're clicking on Margaret's email with the subject line "resignation".

What do you know about the values and ambitions – the true "motivators" – of your people?

This is a person-focused way of thinking. It puts a respect for the individual and their life at the core of your managing style. The logical extension is, of course, that their personal well-being is paramount. If you truly respect them, you'll have the largeness of spirit to let them go willingly. As G.K. Chesterton said, "The way to love anything is to realize that it might be lost." (And as Sting sang, "If you love someone, set them free.")

SMART
DEFINITIONS

"Golden Handshake" (n): that which provides the recipient with just the nest egg he or she needs to leave your company to form that internet start-up or wood-carving business.

The other way to think about retention – a reality check this – is that you may be after a fool's paradise. The very people you fight so hard to hire and retain are precisely those who your competitors want. How can you be surprised if they leave?

If managing employee retention in the past was akin to tending a dam that keeps a reservoir in place, today it is more like managing a river. The object is not to prevent water from flowing out but to control its direction and speed.

Peter Capelli, *The New Deal at Work: Managing the Market-Driven Workforce*

Churn: Smart managers maintain a fresh and committed workforce

All the people come and go, talking of Michelangelo. (T.S. Eliot)

And yet, and yet . . . balance is all: too much retention can be a bad thing.

Some years back, I did some work for an IT department in the insurance industry. The leaders there were concerned about what was happening to values such as loyalty and stability (I told you it was some years back) when such a high proportion of their staff was from the itinerant IT contractor community. After three weeks of interview and workshops, the evidence was clear to me, though it was not what the client expected to hear. The biggest challenge the leadership faced in creating a high-performance workplace was not the fact that young mercenaries came and went with such regularity, but the attitudes and behaviours of

Steve Redgrave

Five gold medals won at consecutive Olympic Games make Steve Redgrave the outstanding athlete in the history of the modern Olympic Games. He has also been world champion a record nine times and is a triple Commonwealth champion. His glittering career is a phenomenal achievement that reflects the unique combination of talent, dedication and ambition that he embodies.

An equally glittering career as a motivational speaker awaits for business people keen to learn how ordinary people can acheive extraordinary things.

the permanent staff who were comfortable, resentful, capricious and insulated from the realities of the outside world.

Churn – or natural attrition as it is sometimes referred to – is the process whereby your company maintains freshness of thinking, openness to change and connection to reality. Organizations are powerful systems – they suck people in and subtly get them to think, talk and act the same. Part of this is a natural and planned by-product of the management of the corporate culture and the "internal brand'. Part of it is the mysterious process of socialization and group think. People have been subject to it for centuries. The downsides of it are obvious: if we're all thinking and talking the same, where does the learning and adaptation to change come from? If we are all of the same standard and we all know each others" level of competence, where does challenge and stretch come from? And if we've all worked here for 30 years, what on earth will be left to talk about at the water fountain?

Churn is good. It can even be designed in by employing contract staff. But it has to be managed.

Churn:

- *Brings in new ideas and perspectives*
  New employees are not like us; they have recent and relevant experience of the real world outside the insulating walls of the organization. Their thinking in conjunction with established ways of doing things might be the catalyst for something entirely new.

- *Provides focus for the corporate culture*
  New employees are the symbols of the values, behaviours and competences that the organization esteems. They can therefore reinforce corporate cultural messages or they can point to a deliberate change in direction. An IT department that appoints a non-technical person from, say, a marketing background as Head of IT is sending big signals to the workforce about what is valued in the changing culture.

Smart things
to say

What are we doing for this
company's tomorrow?

- *Re-energizes the existing workforce*
  Churn is a (not-so) subtle way of keeping everyone on their toes. In itself signals that in an ever-changing world nothing is permanent and nobody should expect comfort and security at all times. Churn is not a threat, still least is it a failure on the part of the organization, but a reflection of how things really are. Life reinvents itself. So should organizations.

No matter how smart you are at attracting and inducting people into your company and, when necessary, managing their exit with everyone's dignity intact, you need to be sure that the workplace you are creating as a manager is a great reality of every day, rather than a great promise you made on the first day.

That's the subject of the next chapter: what sort of workplace can you create that encourages people to decide, every day, to stay with you?

3

Creating a healthy and compelling place to work

A Smart Thing to Know about People

People are living human beings.

They need healthy and compelling places to work, fit for the heart and soul as well as for the bank balance. What one of those might be is the subject of this chapter.

SMART QUOTES

> We are in the formative stages of this revolution of community. But this much we know: success in the Knowledge Era is as much about the spirit of the enterprise as the economics of the business; as much about the positive energy it unleashes as the positive cash flow it creates. We also know that the most valuable knowledge often resides where we are least able to see or control it: on the front lines, at the periphery, with the renegades. Companies that embrace the emergent can tap the logic of knowledge work and the spirit of community. Those that don't will be left behind.
>
> John Seely Brown Vice-President and Chief Scientist of Xerox Corporation

There are two big principles to remember when you are trying to create a great place to work. No matter what you actually end up doing – what practices and packages you create – these two principles are the beliefs that will uphold all your efforts:

1. Human beings are human beings – so treat them as such

This in turn requires you to understand how human beings are, how they operate, what their needs are, and what makes them work more effectively.

For the greater part of the 20th century, people have studied what makes organizations work, what its constituent parts are, and how to combine them effectively together.

If I asked you to draw your organization, you would be able to do so easily. You'd probably draw a chart which shows how the various responsibilities and disciplines are shared across your company. Or you'd draw a process chart which demonstrates how inputs lead to outputs, how doing certain things in certain order creates customer satisfaction and positive return on investment for the organization towards its mission.

My suggestion is that nowadays it is the manager's job to show the same level of understanding regarding human beings.

The trouble is with this is that too many managers think that "understanding human beings" is the remit of qualified psychologists or, worse, God. But we instinctively, over the years, build up a wealth of knowledge about human nature – our own and others. Whether this understanding is absolutely accurate and detailed or not, or whether we'd be asked to lecture on it at Harvard Medical School, doesn't matter. Does it work for you, that's what matters.

Any simple working model or series of theses (like the Six Smart Things to Know About People which constitute the spine of this book) will help you reflect on whether what you are doing is working well, given that the person you are managing is a human being and not a "human resource" or "personnel unit".

And the reason it is so necessary to do this work is because many processes and systems in management have been designed with "human resources" or "personnel units" in mind, rather than the complex, unpredictable living organisms that people are.

When I wrote *Sacred Business* (Capstone, 1997) with Heather Campbell, the model we worked with there was that human beings have four interconnecting aspects: mental, emotional, physical and spiritual. It is a simple model, but nothing I have experienced in life since writing that book has shown me that the model is "wrong" or "insufficient".

And if you were to debate the model over dinner with your friends, you'd probably think: well, yes, good, I agree, people do have four interconnecting aspects: mental, emotional, physical and spiritual. But so what?

The so what is that these same people who have these four aspects are in your company. You manage human beings who have not just mental and physical but emotional and spiritual aspects too. And they have, to varying degrees, mental and physical but emotional and spiritual needs to satisfy.

What implications does this immediately have for how you relate to your people?

One of the main management mantras of the last century was "getting the best out of people". The management mantra of the new century could be "getting the best out of the whole person". But how can you get the best out of a human being unless you have an understanding of what a human being is?

SMART QUOTES

It becomes critical to understand what issues drive all humans and which metaphors speak to those issues. There are seven human emotions: love, hate, joy, sorrow, anger, passion, and fear. The Panda Bear is the only other animal that exhibits all seven of these emotions. Pandas had a significant resonance in eastern societies, but there was an overwhelming response when they were introduced to the west.

Watts Wacker

2. Recognize that your people are working for you in the early part of the 21st century

The world of work is a profoundly different place from that one of 15 years ago. Society has undergone major shifts – the rise of the role and number of women in the workplace and the very existence of the work/life balance concept are just two examples. The needs of workers has changed too. People have a rich and rewarding life outside work; they don't expect their organizations to get unfairly in the way of that. They may even expect their organizations to help them manage their lives better . . .

These two principles have produced some interesting experiments in how organizations treat their people.

I choose not to blindly follow old beliefs about people at work, e.g.:
- people should keep their personal lives at home
- give people an inch and they'll take a mile
- fairness means treating everyone exactly the same
- flexible working and other benefit programmes can make people happier, but not more productive
- being "present" equals being "productive"
- hours at work equals performance

Dr L. Duxbury (Carleton University, School of Business) and Dr C. Higgins (University of Western Ontario, School of Business)

Smart things to say

Sanity Incorporated?

SAS Institute is a $1 billion software company in North Carolina, which

was termed Sanity Incorporated by *Fast Company* magazine in its January 1999 issue. Are they setting new standards for creating a healthy and balanced place to work? It certainly sounds idyllic:

> *In a quiet corner of North Carolina, there's a place that contradicts most of the assumptions of modern business. In an era of relentless pressure, this place is an oasis of calm. In an age of frantic competition, this place is methodical and clearheaded. In a world of free agency, signing bonuses, and stock options, this is a place where loyalty matters more than money.*

The list of benefits people at SAS Institute can expect include:

- a 35 hour full-time work week (the recorded receptionist voice mail at 5.00 p.m. says "most people have gone home now");

- live piano music in the cafeteria;

- unlimited soda, coffee, tea, and juice;

- one week's paid vacation between Christmas and New Year's Day

- a 36,000 sq. ft on site gym that includes two full-length basketball courts, ping-pong tables, a dance studio and a skylit yoga room;

- workout clothes laundered over night free of charge;

- two on-site and one off-site day care facilities;

- an on-site health clinic staffed with six nurses and two physicians;

- free health insurance;

- casual dress every day (except in client meetings);

- elder-care advice and referrals;

- on-site massages several times a week;

- all family benefits extended to domestic partners, regardless of sexual orientation;

- unlimited sick days, and use of sick days to care for sick family members; and

- and 22.5 tons of M&Ms every year given free to staff, distributed every Wednesday.

It is not unusual to find flexible working arrangements (people have choice over the hours they work to fit domestic responsibilities) in companies now. We are not far away from paid paternity leave as standard. Some large organizations offer holi-conferencing, which opens up the company's teleconferencing facilities to connect on-the-road staff members and their distant families during public holidays. Some companies offer privacy rooms which allow returned-to-work-but-still-breast-feeding mothers to be with their babies. Still others have some form of concierge service. Did your dishwasher break down last night? The dishwasher company has promised to send an engineer "sometime before noon". You can't afford to be away from your cubicle that long, can you? Never fear. The corporate concierge will come to your desk, pick up your house keys, wait for said engineer, oversee the completion of the work, leave your apartment safe and secure and return the keys to you by the close of the day. No worries.

Many managers would be horrified at such lists of benefits, seeing them as distractions from the "important stuff" of actually doing the work. If people genuinely have the characteristics of Theory X (see below: Smart people to have on your side – Douglas McGregor), then the SAS Institute would clearly never get anything done (like making a billion dollars for example). So how does SAS prevent people from taking advantage of its largess? What if its people decided to spend all day playing ping-pong?

"I can't imagine", says Senior Vice President John Sall, "that playing ping-pong would be more interesting than work . . ."

Now that's a Theory Y view if ever I heard one.

SMART
PEOPLE
TO HAVE
ON YOUR
SIDE

Douglas McGregor (1906–64)

McGregor's book *The Human Side of Enterprise* outlined a theory which suggested management behaviour could stem from two opposing views of the inherent motivations of human beings. Theory X asserted that people don't like work, need to be coerced towards organizational goals and prefer to be directed since they don't like to take responsibility for their actions and destiny. Theory Y suggested that work is a natural part of life, that people will seek responsibility under the right conditions, and are bright and perhaps largely underutilized.

A Smart thing to remember about life–work balance

Innovative programmes like the ones at SAS, and the other companies mentioned in this chapter, can apparently simultaneously increase efficiency and productivity, improve the lives of their employees, and reinforce loyalty and goodwill towards the corporation.

But initiatives like these must come from the heart rather than from the balance sheet. It needs to be part of the expression of the company's integrity and mission, rather than a clever management ploy:

Creating a family-friendly company

This article from the HBR website shows how far some companies could go to minimize the disruptions caused by the life work dilemma – and, as the last point suggests, actually save the company money in the process.

Address the special needs of new and expecting parents
The first step is to make sure your company has a generous maternity/paternity leave policy – and that employees who do take time off around childbirth aren't subtly penalized when they return to work. Time pressures, financial worries and unpredictable work schedules are particular concerns for expecting parents and employees with very young children. Companies can help by offering programs such as parenting and child-development education and home visitation by health professionals, and by making it easier for new mothers to continue nursing their infants by providing a place for them to express and store breast milk at work. These programs have been shown to decrease health care costs for mothers and infants while cutting down on absenteeism.

Offer flexible work schedules
In one study, 30% of the employees surveyed reported difficulty getting time off to attend school activities. Nearly 25% reported resistance from managers when asking for time to attend parent–teacher conferences. Flexible start and stop times can often alleviate this problem. If that isn't possible, another alternative is "release time", a designated number of paid hours that employees can use to attend parent conferences, participate in school activities, or even accompany their children on their first day of school.

Bring the school to the office
Sometimes the nature of the business makes it impossible to permit flex time or release time; an assembly line, for example, can't function except when it's fully staffed. So Ridgeview Company, operator of a factory in North Carolina, works with local schools to schedule 15-minute teacher conferences at the workplace, which employees can attend during work hours. Parents are able to stay on top of their children's performance at school with minimum disruption to the company's business.

Provide programs for employees' children

How many parents disappear from the job during school vacations? Companies can boost efficiency and reduce absenteeism during these periods by establishing programs for children. Eli Lilly (Indianapolis) runs a summer science camp for the children of Indianapolis-based employees. John Hancock Financial Services (Boston) runs a program called "Kids-to-Go", which takes employees' children on area field trips during school vacation.

Offer training and resources

Sometimes the hardest part of parenting is the intangible worry – like not knowing where to turn for help and information. Create a supportive culture in your organization through guidance. Sponsor lunchtime-speaker programs with education and child-care experts. Pay for employee subscriptions to parenting and education newsletters. Set up a library with parenting books and videos and other information sources.

Measure results

WFD, Inc., a Boston-based consulting firm specializing in labour issues, has developed a cost–benefit model that can be used to measure the impact of corporate initiatives. Companies can use it to measure increased performance, employee retention, stress reduction, and reduced absenteeism. For example, according to the Work & Life 2000 study, John Hancock Financial Services found that "the payback for every dollar invested in family-friendly policies was $3.83", resulting in a total savings of $573,860 for one year.

Like any program, a work/family initiative must be supported by the organization's culture to be effective. Employees shouldn't feel that they'll be seen in a negative light by their co-workers or superiors if they decide to take advantage of a family-friendly policy. What's more, cautions Rima Shore, piecemeal programs and short-term solutions won't work. The commitment to child development and education should be compound, not limited to parents of school-age children. One way to promote an accepting environment is to widen the appeal of the program so that all employees can participate. For example, consider partnering with local schools by setting up employee volunteer opportunities.

Source: www.hbsp.harvard.edu – article edited from the original

What distinguishes the best companies, however, is not that they recognize how important balance is to attracting talent – it's how they create such balance in their organizations. Not long ago, any decent listing of "great places to work" would identify companies large and small that offered a preset "Chinese menu" of programs for balancing work and life: maternity and paternity leave, company-sponsored day care and elder care, regular retreats and periodic sabbaticals, flextime and even flexplace. In the new economy, the kind of balance that attracts people isn't a set of programs. Rather, it's a way of doing business. Balance is deeply embedded in the company's core – a compelling part of its corporate DNA.

Robert B. Reich

It could be argued, moreover, that it is fitting for an organization to give something positive back to its community in the form of balanced lives and supported children. The last generation has shown how much negative energy can come out of organizations – stress, broken marriages, disrupted parent/child relationships – all in the name of free capitalism.

Five ways you can create a workplace that people want to leave

1. Never show yourself. Be absent and/or unavailable. When you are cornered by staff, look at your watch a lot and sigh

2. Tell people what to do and how. Discourage flexibility of approach.

3. Fail to match work to competence; give people the wrong job.

4. Leave people out of the loop. Never involve them in decisions or problem-solving. Dump solutions on them without context or background.

5. Always remember and demonstrate that your people are children or criminals and thank God you are there to stop them stealing the carpet tiles . . .

Perhaps the next generation of healthy organizations could begin to redress the balance.

The work–life balance thing at a personal level

Here are some principles you could bear in mind in your own personal quest for life–work balance:

1. *You can't create balance without considering the elements that we are trying to bring into balance.*

Many people bust a gut trying to satisfy the demands of work and life and wonder why they don't feel in balance – it's because they've left themselves out of the equation. This metaphor we hold of a see-saw attempting to balance work and home life is flawed – there's more than two areas of your life to be balanced. Where do you fit into your life? Too many business executives have left themselves out of the work–home–self triangle.

SMART
ANSWERS
TO TOUGH
QUESTIONS

Q: How can I generate more commitment in my people?

A: First locate the obvious: that everyone is committed to something. Find what that is in each of your people, and respond to it . . .

2. *Balance is subjective and changes over time.*

There is no right or wrong balance to aim for, only what works for you at this moment in time. What is a good balance for me may not be an acceptable balance for you.

To achieve an optimum balance between your work, self and home, you have to work towards, and make continual adjustments towards, compromise. Sometimes, inevitably work has to take priority; other times your self or your home does.

3. *Your intuition rather than your diary tells you when you're out of balance.*

You could point to your organizer and prove to me that your life can't be out of balance because you spent eight days with your family last month. That's one story, certainly. Only your heart will tell you whether your presence in those weekends with the children was largely physical rather than emotional. Your body may have been present, but your thoughts back in the office.

4. *Balance is about saying no.*

Sometimes you'll have to say "no" at work, at other times you have to say "no" at home. It's also about saying no to those things you originally said yes to – which is a bit like the process that goes on when you're trying to come to terms with addiction. You can't just go cold turkey and stop doing the things you said yes to – like that obsessive working schedule. You need to come to terms with what it was about that obsessive working schedule that attracted you so much and had such a hold on you. *That* is what you need to say no to.

5. *Balance requires us to work in those areas in which we are most uncomfortable.*

Balance isn't just about time management: there could be elements of your being which are out of balance. Think of the numbers person whose left-brain logical powers become strongly developed at the expense of the emotional or intuitive side of their character. Coming into balance would mean developing right-brain aspects. Necessarily this is going to be an uncomfortable process because he or she is now working with areas which feel new or very different.

6. *It is difficult to achieve balance without looking at the bigger context of your life.*

When attempting to balance the conflicting demands of children, work and your personal well-being, questions of purpose often arise. We move from "What should I do next?" to "Why am I doing this at all?" or "To what end am I working in this way?" Do not be surprised if people around you for whom work–life balance is an important thing suddenly start adding new activities rather than simply taking things away. They may well express an interest in performing charity, community or other works of service to others. Consideration of purpose often calls people to give something back to the world rather than looking to only take from it.

KILLER
QUESTIONS

How can we be sure that our benefits – flextime, career-learning, etc. – are both available to and being taken by all? How can we ensure that this is seen not just a perk of the job for "senior" people when they've "earned" the right to it?

The little secret: the shadow side of the work–life balance thing

Here's a thought. Imagine getting everyone in your company to answer the question: "Who believes home life is more stressful than work life?"

Certainly research coming out of the USA suggests that for more and more people, the workplace – for so long seen as the exploitative hindrance to "real" life – is actually a haven from the fractious children, household chores emotional minefields waiting at home. Where else can you get such a sense of accomplishment, fulfilment, and camaraderie? Not at home when the kids are whining because they haven't seen enough of you and the dishwasher's broken down again.

> People aren't cutting back their hours. In fact, both spouses in a typical two-job family are spending more and more time at work—not necessarily because there's more to do, or even because they're afraid of losing their jobs. They're fleeing the pressures and increasing uncertainties of home life and escaping to work, where they can feel in control, and maybe even have some fun.
>
> Arlie Russell Hochschild, *The Time Bind: When Work Becomes Home and Home Becomes Work*

Depressing eh? Not exactly the outcome that SAS had in mind, I'd guess.

What does your team think, and what could you put in place as a result?

The work–life balance thing at a team level

How can you as a manager create a healthy place to work by having the people who work there live healthy, balanced lives. Certainly there are initiatives and benefits your company can create – SAS has shown that. But there is important work you can do every day to make work life balance a reality. You will need to demonstrate sensitivity and you will need to begin by building a bond of trust.

SMART
PEOPLE
TO HAVE
ON YOUR
SIDE

Andy Law

Though only five years old, St Luke's Communications has become one of the most talked about advertising agencies in the UK. It is an experiment in what a healthy and compelling organization could become. St Luke's is the only co-owned venture in the advertising industry. It wins numerous awards — though it doesn't enter contests — and it has increased its profits eightfold. Chairman and co-founder Andy Law attributes the firm's success to its determination to continuously reinvent itself in a world populated by dot-coms and mega-ad agencies.

St Luke's intends to revolutionize the way business is done and provide a credible alternative to the capitalism of both the old economy and the new. Law sees business as

> the most powerful force at work today . . . [it] can treat you as well or as badly as it chooses. Yet we devote our lives unthinkingly to it, giving our knowledge, creativity and sweat without regard to its true value.

To bring back some measure of balance to life and work, St Luke's has chosen to turn its back on many business conventions and habits.

To this end, St Luke's pushes its people to take enormous risks, both in their creative work and in their personal development (a recent HBR article about him was called "Creating the most frightening company on earth"). As Law says: "We're fundamentally convinced that there is a connection between co-ownership, creativity, collaboration, and competitive advantage."

On the back cover of his book, *Open Minds: 21st Century Business Lessons and Innovations from St Lukes*, Law offers the following advice:

Ten ways to create a revolution in your company

1. Ask yourself what you really want out of life.

2. Ask yourself what really matters to you.

3. Give all your workclothes to Oxfam and wear what you feel is really you.

4. Talk to people (even those you don't like) about 1 and 2. (You should be feeling very uncomfortable now. You may even be sick. This is normal.)

5. Give up something you most need at work (desk, company car, etc.).

6. Trust everyone you meet. Keep every agreement you make. (You should be feeling a little better now.)

7. Undergo a group experience (anything goes – parachuting, holidaying).

8. Rewrite your business plan to align all of the above with your customers.

9. Draw a line on the office floor and invite everyone to a brave new world

10. Share everything you do and own fairly with everyone that crosses that line.

(You should be feeling liberated. Soon you will have, in this order, the following: grateful customers, inspired employees, friendly communities, money).

1. Talk about it

Give the subject of work–life balance legitimacy. Much of Shadow 3, supported by a whole raft of macho-management-dominated corporate cultures, excluded the relevance of people's lives outside work. Work and life were separate boxes (in the same way that heads and hands in the individual were valued to the exclusion of their hearts and spirit). What people did (or could not do) in the privacy of their own homes was nothing to do with the company. Worse still, anyone in such a culture who showed signs of stress or breakdown would be considered weak and be made a candidate for expulsion in the next round of redundancy.

If you talk about work–life balance, you make it acceptable as a goal. You also allow discussion of what gets in the way of achieving it, and what all of us could do to make it more likely.

Make it clear that your success criteria include two main elements: (a) business performance and (b) staff fulfilment. Underline that you will

Smart questions to consider and to ask your team if "flexible" working becomes a possibility

- How will we maintain a sense of community and connection if some of us are not always in the office?

- How do we maintain fairness and minimize challenges of favouritism?

- How will we deal with voiced or unvoiced, realistic or otherwise, feelings of envy from office-bound staff?

- Who's really interested in working from home or elsewhere? Who prefers the ritual of coming to the office?

- Who has to be here, when and why?

- When communicating by conference call, how will we compensate for the loss of visual data like body language, facial expression, etc.?

- Are we sure that those working out of the office have the technical resources to support them – and the training to exploit those resources?

- Do those who will be working from home have the skills and discipline to separate the demands of work and life? Or will they be tempted, for example, to work all hours?

- How will they bring the same structures and ritual (e.g. chatting at the water cooler) to their working day at home?

- How will I as a manager measure the performance of those who work from elsewhere?

- Given that we will lose many of the informal, spontaneous meetings, how will we in review meetings balance the need to be both focused and informal or social?

- How will we educate our customer and suppliers in the new reality that some staff will not be physically in the corporate building?

- What might we learn in time about changing work practices in the office from those who work outside it?

consider yourself a failure if only the former is achieved and ask your people's help in succeeding in both domains.

2. Personalize it

Since work–life balance is a subjective thing and shifts over time, you must make every effort to understand the demands that each individual faces outside the workplace. Blanket initiatives must give way to flexible, personalized solutions. This does not mean gaining casual knowledge of hobbies or pets' names, but a deeper understanding of the roles that people play outside the workplace and even the personal purpose and principles. What matters to them, and how can it be acknowledged (or even used) in the workplace.

3. Set compelling goals, but loose boundaries

Your job as a manager is to set high standards for achieving stretch goals which move the organization towards its vision. But there is little in your remit which says you must tell your people *how* they are to achieve those goals. Getting out of the way of your people allows their creativity to develop (though clearly you need to be available as a coach when required). It also allows them to set their own constraints – or reinvent old ones. Shadow 3 constraints include the principles that we all work the same hours (roughly 9–5 and usually Monday to Friday). If you never challenge the legitimacy of such principles, you'll only ever be reinventing the past as a manager.

Why would you bother with all this "healthy company" stuff?

Pick your answer:

1. *For profit.*
   You'd do it for money. It makes logical, pragmatic business sense. It's cheaper to retain someone than lose and replace them.

2. *For the performance improvements you'd get.*
   I can tell when I'm observing a team which is out of balance or "unhealthy'

   - more effort than productivity;

   - unresolved tension between members;

   - a lack of empathy;

   - tunnel vision + tunnel acting;

   - lack of passion;

   - easily side-tracked;

   - guilt and doubt over those areas which are neglected;

   - emotionally and mentally drained by the strain of trying to get something done in such an environment.

3. *Because the labour market requires it.*
   The best knowledge workers know how valuable they are. The money they receive is only part of their reward package, and they could get the same money elsewhere. What they are looking for is companies which make an effort to provide a great place to work.

4. *Because you're a human being too.*
   And there's no reason to step out of that just because you're a manager now and someone, somewhere once conditioned you to think that management is about playing hardball tough guy/gal.

Building a humane working culture at Abbot Mead Vickers

One of the many things we've picked up from the Third Shadow is that the world of business is a hard, macho, cold-blooded, ruthless place in which to operate. Kindness is for wimps. Management is for bastards.

But an article in *Management Today* of September 2000 suggests that at least one successful manager is providing a blueprint for capturing the hearts and minds of staff by – steady now – being nice to them.

Peter Mead is the 60-year-old co-founder of the biggest ad agency in the UK. Here's his recipe for treating a company like "a family":

- Be the glue that keeps the company together.

- See and be seen. Enquire into people's wellbeing.

- Clarify and communicate convictions, beliefs, principles.
  You won't need courage or bravado then, since you won't be operating in a vacuum

- Minimize fear and anxiety.
  Instead give people the momentum they need by allowing them access to the information and resources they need to be naturally concerned for the health of the company

- Keep the HR department small.
  Because the people who hire and manage should be responsible for their staff: if you have to sack someone, it's a failure for you as much as them.

- Don't act like "a manager".
  Be a human being like every one else.

> Smart things to know about being nice

How do you know if yours is a healthy and compelling place to work?

Ask these questions of your people, regularly enough to detect any changes or patterns:

1. What gets in the way of work being fun for you?

2. How often this month have you been recognized and thanked for the work you do? Is that enough?

3. How often this month has your life outside the confines of this workplace been acknowledged as a real and legitimate part of your existence?

4. How often have you been engaged in formal conversations about the purpose, strategy, goals and health of this department and or company? Is that enough?

5. Do you feel that you are listened to and that your opinion is valued?

6. Do you know what's going on in this company? What are you missing?

7. Are you feeling like a mature human being here or a cog in the machine?

8. Are you growing and developing in your current role?

9. Do you know what your goals are and do you have the resources to achieve them?

10. Do you respect and enjoy working with your colleagues?

11. Do you feel adequately and fairly compensated for the time and talent you invest in this company?

You as a compelling role model: why should people be led by you?

There is one final critical link in the twisty ladder which is the DNA of a healthy company, and that is you. One of the chief conduits for people's connection to their work is their relationship with the boss. Part of that relationship is governed by your competence in setting key managerial skills such as delegation, goal-setting, performance measurement and communication. But a larger part of it runs deeper than your expertise in techniques. It is to do with what I called Shadow 1 in the first chapter: the personal shadow. It is to do with character. It is to do with you being a compelling role model, a trusting and trustworthy person who strives for integrity.

Hypocrisy and the challenge of walking your talk

It's not "walk the talk"; it's actually "walk *your* talk". "Walk the talk" doesn't come close to conveying how very personal this is. It's not an exhortation to model the organizational's "talk", it's not about how well you can toe the corporate line. It's about who you are – and whether the person we experience is the same one that we were promised . . . "Walk *your* talk" is about taking responsibility for what you commit to.

Smart things to say

In seeking all this purpose, people will look for an aligned workplace, one where there is no conflict between what it says it is and what it actually is. This conflict arises from the difference between the espoused values on the Vision and Mission Statement up on the reception wall, and the "real" values that are lived out in the day-to-day reality. It arises also from the difference between what a leader says she'll do and what she actually does.

This conflict is commonplace in all of life, not just at work. I just recently heard a journalist state that the purpose of his newspaper's work was to "root out hypocrisy". It's why the Blair government's strategy of spin is both its triumph and may well be its destruction. People are highly attuned to look for the difference between a promise made and the delivery of a promise. The cynicometer is very sensitive.

And people at their work have had too much experience of these sorts of conflict for you to be smart enough to get away with it. That managers are hypocritical is in the "meaning set" of apocryphal Bosses in the collective consciousness – that bosses can't be trusted to do as they say is part of the promise of Shadow 3. In other words, people will be expecting you to fulfil that promise, model that characteristic, be a hypocrite. The balance is set against you before you start. You'll have to work very hard even to get the balance level.

What is at stake when you allow hypocrisy to arise is the credibility of your organization, on one hand, and your personal integrity on the other.

Integrity

The inevitably of being a hypocrite is that there is always something to hide.

Either you're hiding from what you said, from what you promised, from what you declared to the world about what would happen. Or you're hiding your "true self" from the world, because you said one thing and, for whatever political reason, for whatever personal benefit, you need to live that promise out, even though what you promised was a deceit or a mistake.

Managers struggle with these issues day after day. The organization makes a decision which you need to implement, even though it's against your principles or values. You make a promise to John that you'll do that much-postponed appraisal meeting with him this coming Friday – and then you're called by your own boss to an urgent strategy session. Your integrity is constantly being tested.

When you make a promise, the words you use have power, have reality, they are not just air, not just sound waves, they bring a world forth that would not have been there had you said those words. When your behaviour breaks a promise, that is an equally powerful act. It brings forth another world, a world in which what you say cannot be trusted.

Not walking your talk is a terribly stressful way to live, because at some level you're always scared you'll be found out (and you can be sure the spotlight that projects the Shadows will always find you out at some stage). You'll be found out for being a fake, a con-artist, for not being up to the job. What fear! What tension! Think how much energy you're using to keep from being found out which you could be using for something much more positive and constructive.

Having integrity, on the other hand, is when there is nothing left to hide.

Getting complete – maintaining and regaining integrity

It is almost inevitable that people will judge that you have lost integrity at some point in your career as a manager. What can you do to maintain integrity and to regain it when it appears to be at risk?

Here are three main pieces of advice. The first two are what you need to do generally and consistently over time to manage people's expectation of what's realistic and possible. The other one is what you need to do when you've failed to keep a promise.

1. Set the context

Explain to people the complexity, contradictions and unpredictabilities that go with having your job – not so that you gain their sympathy or pity, not so you have something to excuse your inadequacies but so you can help them become mature members of the organizational system. Too often people drop into simplistic and lazy thinking that if only their boss would do one or two things differently, everything would be fine. Shadow 3 tells people that Bosses know exactly what to do and have all the power, but sometimes, on a whim and for the hell of it, they act capriciously to torment their followers. Challenge this fantasy, and connect people to the true complexity of organizational life.

2. Generate trustworthiness

There are some simple principles to remember in developing trust between you and your colleagues:

- *Know yourself*
  Watts Wacker describes a brand as a promise and applies that understanding to individuals. *You* are a brand – you are a promise of value added, or accomplishment achieved, or security embodied, of love given. The point is that you can't keep a promise if who you are – the promise-maker – keeps shifting. Consistency is the bedrock of trust.

- *Explain who you are and what you stand for*
  In which case people around you will know by what standards, measures or principles to judge you (and judge you they will, whether you communicate with them or not).

- *Demonstrate clearly what it is you share with – and how you are different from – your team members*
  A vision, a view of life, a set of objectives, a sense of humour. People trust people who are like them.

- *Be around so that you can be observed*
  By all means have virtual meetings by email; but accept the reality that "face-mail" is where trust is born

- *Don't act*
  Be authentic, be yourself

- *Be consistent*
  Make compelling promises and act accordingly after doing so. If you realize you cannot keep the promise:
  – revoke it and make another one
  – ameliorate the effects of not keeping the promise
  – ask what you can do to minimize the inconvenience to the person concerned.

- *Be honest* – which has two elements:
  – tell the truth
  – be open about your shortcomings

- *Operate from the stance of "What can I give?"* Rather than "What can I get?"

- *Put your political power on the line as the façade it is:*
  In other words, when you screw up, say sorry.

3. Apologize

Say sorry when any promise you make is broken. There is more than one level to this.

- At base you need to tell the truth about what happened – without excuse or interpretation. This is a signal that you have seen exactly what the other does. "John: I'm sorry. I said that we would have your appraisal meeting on Friday. But I went into another meeting instead."

- Tell the other how that breach of trust makes you feel. Why? Because it helps people believe you when you report your experience. (If you tell yourself that you feel nothing about breaking your promises then you're living up to Shadow 3 and you are a manipulator who is scared that one day you'll be found out.)

- Don't give excuses unless they are demanded. Even then they should be proffered for what they are. Excuses are your stories, your sales pitches for yourself. Having integrity means being able to stand up from behind all that stuff. All that matters is that what you said would happen didn't happen. All that matters is that next time it *will* happen. Besides, what presents itself as a powerful excuse to you ("My boss told me to go the strategy meeting") rarely has the same impact

Be that which you want

The search for new management paradigms is not a recent phenomenon. Management writers and thinkers have continuously strived for better methods of working to achieve time, cost and quality objectives. Nor have they been averse for looking to the lessons of history and ancient wisdom for inspirational material (e.g. The Management Secrets of Attila the Hun; The Tao of Leadership). Here's eight commandments from just one such attempt, which suggests the Holy Bible might be one of the first management how-to texts.

Towards managerial efficacy: back to 2,000-year-old guiding principles:

1. Do not be conceited, boastful or self-righteous.

2. Do not provoke one another. Avoid provocation.

3. Do not envy one another. Rejoice with others who have achieved something for the organization.

4. Forgive: The guiding principle is to forgive and to accept a wayward person back into the organization through coaching.

5. Carry one another's burden. Assist others who are in need of help to alleviate their burden.

6. Be humble. Come down to people's level

7. Do not make comparison. People are all different. However, when we make comparison, we highlight our differences, and when we highlight our differences, we build barriers and walls. Thus, when we accept and appreciate our differences we become one united and harmonious vessel.

8. Do the best you can, as much as you can, to as many as you can

Low Sui Pheng

on the other. What an excuse means to you will probably not mean the same to them ("My boss told me to go the strategy meeting" translates easily to "You don't care about my personal development nor me as a human being").

- Admit something about yourself as a tendency or pattern ("I keep taking too much on because I love to be busy. This I now see is at the expense of my connection to people like you. I need to stop doing that").

- Ask permission to make a commitment to whatever needs to happen next (a rescheduled meeting with John, for example). This stage clarifies whether the other is ready to listen, to reaccommodate your promises. If not, you need to be truthful further.

- Make the commitment. And this time remember that you are creating the future – and that breaking a promise gives everyone the excuse to retreat into and live from the past.

Shadow 3 mythology – maintained by an industry of leadership training – would like to tell you that you should never open yourself as honestly as I've just described. Some of it would even have you hide your mistakes (a great tactic, really, for never having to apologize). But believe me, the political power that is sustained by sham and deceit is done so at huge cost to the personal power that is sustained by integrity and authenticity. The stress of fearing you'll be found out will wear you down over the years – and then you'll be found out anyway. Don't waste

SMART QUOTES

Years ago, I earned a black belt in karate – which is how I learned the concept of "relaxed focus". The typical businessperson experiences 170 interactions per day (phone calls, hallway conversations, emails) and has a backlog of 200–300 hours of uncompleted work. How do you relax and focus amid so much chaos? You need ruthless clarity. Ask two simple questions about everything that comes across the transom: What is it? Is it actionable? If it's not actionable, then you eliminate it or incubate it. If it is actionable, then you ask, What's the next step? You can do it, delegate it, or defer it. I call this "next-step management".

That doesn't mean always working on the "most important" stuff first. There are few occasions when you have the energy, the tools, and the time needed to work on your highest-priority items. Sometimes the most appropriate thing to do, if you have 10 free minutes, is to water your plants.

David Allen, US personal productivity guru

your time. Be real. You are a human being who makes mistakes, no matter what joke of a job title they gave you in HR. Apologize.

Healthy organizations demand that you step out of Shadow 3 management – the distant, capricious, inconsistent, impersonal – and strive to create an environment which encourages and rewards human talent.

To do this, you'll need to make sure you understand the new rules of attraction . . .

4

Connecting

A Smart Thing to Know about People

People are fundamentally creative creatures – they create their lives and work from how they think, talk and act. In this constant whirl of thinking, talking and acting, people make things mean things. Where no meaning exists, they'll create one. Your job is to establish an environment which allows your people to establish and follow the most constructive and compelling meanings.

This chapter examines how you can connect people to you, to the mission and purpose of the organization and to the outside world – and therefore maintain a constructively meaningful place to work.

I believe participation is not a choice. You can't avoid including people, because life is about the creation of new systems through relationships and through inclusion. It's also true that leaders who have worked in autocratic corporations realize that it's not a model of leadership that you can link to issues of sustainability. If you're interested in creating sustainable growth, sustainable productivity, sustainable morale, you can't do that through autocracy. You can work the numbers for a quarter or a half a year, you can drive people to exhaustion for a few months or a couple of years. But if you haven't focused on creating capacity in the organization, it will die through those efforts. So it's not only in times of stability or rapid change that we see the failures of autocracy, I would say. If you're trying to create a healthy organization, one that can sustain itself over time, simply legislating and dictating behaviour and outcomes doesn't work at all.

Margaret Wheatley

This chapter looks at the subject of communication as the energy that connects people together, and thus moves us from isolation towards unity.

There are three dimensions of connection that this chapter examines:

1. As a manager you need to connect effectively with your people, not just so that they understand what you are asking of them, but also that they feel compelled to take action on your request. In itself, that requires that you are constantly reinventing a level of trust between you all. Trust happens more quickly between people who see and know each other. Communicating regularly – in all sorts of structures from one-to-ones to departmental awaydays – is a channel for creating that trust.

2. You and your people need to live and work in an environment where

you are connected to each other so that they know and respect each other; have all the information and resources they need to accomplish their jobs with a minimum of judgment, blame and envy; are connected to the corporate purpose and goals and, finally, are connected to what is going on outside the organization which might provide a context for what is going on within it

SMART QUOTES
"The most important things in life aren't things."

Anon

3. You need to connect your people to the stories they tell about themselves, so with that added awareness they can consciously choose to recreate the past or to invent a new future

Standpoint 1: connecting people to you

What are the dynamics of trust-building? On pages 90–93, we listed various behaviours and habits which are most likely to be interpreted by others as worthy of their trust. Here we continue that theme, by suggesting that there are ways you can communicate your trustworthiness.

Of course, you don't tell someone that you're trustworthy; trust is something that they read into you – it is something they sense in how you communicate with them.

Communication is a negotiation of meaning.

I'll send a message out to you ("Please step into my office") with the intention that you receive it with a certain meaning ("I want to discuss your performance this week"). You make the message mean something, which might be what I intend (e.g. "He wants to see me to discuss my performance this week – great") or might be something subtly or entirely different ("He wants to see me to give me the sack – oh no!").

Note in this simple example, the *meaning* comes from the mind of the audience – you – and is not inherent in the message itself. Even if I send you a message which is very "clear" ("Please come into my office because I want to discuss your performance this week and nothing else, honestly") you might still take the meaning "He wants to see me to give me the sack – oh no!" if the history of our relationship has little trust, or if you interpret my facial expressions and tone of voice in certain ways.

But the thing to remember is that the meaning is in the audience and not in your message. And unfortunately, in communication terms, if the audience takes a certain meaning away from the communication, then they "win", no matter what you intended. It's a bit like customer service – if the customer says the service is poor, then the service is poor. Better to perform service, and communication, that minimizes the chances of your meaning being misunderstood.

The following advice is focused largely on you as an influencer – but our intention is that you take "influence" to mean anything you do when you try to persuade someone of your point of view is something you are doing whether you are up on stage in front of 300 people with a 30-slide Powerpoint presentation, or whether you are sitting down around a table trying to persuade your team to consider Plan B rather than Plan A. The same principles apply.

KILLER QUESTIONS

What do I intend to mean to my audience?

And since the audience is the final arbiter of your meaning, we start with consideration of the audience.

So, bring to mind an influence you want to have over someone – whether formal presentation or informal meeting.

- What do you want your audience to do, or think, or feel as a result of this meeting?

- What are you offering – an idea, a tool, a promise – that is worthy of them changing from their current state of doing, thinking and feeling to the one you want?

- How will you know that that is happening?

- Who exactly is your audience? How many? What mix of knowledge and experience is in the room with you?

- What do they know – or think they know – about the subject on which you are influencing them? How could you use these assumptions and prejudices to help your case?

- What common ground do you share with your audience?

- What above else do you want them to know about you and your subject?

Now think about the moment of influence itself. Whether you are delivering a presentation in a conference hall or chatting to a colleague over lunch, your audience will be assessing you along five dimensions: intensity, credibility, orientation, mechanics and semantics.

Each of these dimensions answers a question that is being asked somewhere in the conscious or subconscious mind:

KILLER QUESTIONS

What was my impact?

Dimension 1: intensity

Question being asked: Does this person seem to care about what they are saying?

Intensity is about your emotional connection to the material you are delivering, to the subject about which you are attempting to influence people. This is the dimension that can make the most disinterested audience interested, because there is nothing quite so compelling as someone who is passionate about their subject. Passion – intensity – comes from inside someone – it is an access to and symbol of what makes someone unique. Without that confirmation of someone's authenticity, you may as well be reciting someone else's lines. The sight of someone reading a text during a presentation, for example, is disheartening not just because it displays a lack of preparation, but precisely there is such a gap between the person speaking and what the audience heard. There is no connection.

If you are not connected emotionally to your subject, then either act as if you are (only advisable if you are a consummate performer otherwise people will see the join and you'll fail on Dimension 2) or find something in the subject that you can connect to. Or simply get someone else to do the presentation or the conversation. Because if what you are speaking about doesn't seem to matter to you, why should it matter to anyone else?

Dimension 2: credibility

Question being asked: Is this person someone I trust?

Credibility is the dimension that reassures your audience that you are a credible advocate for or model of your subject. Can you yourself do or say what you imply they have to do? Are you knowledgeable on the subject? Is your argument watertight?

Credibility is also about your ease of communication – are you relaxed (physically and mentally); do you have the confidence to get to the point and say what you mean; do you look like a human being (or a rigid robot); do you speak with a recognizably human voice (or is what you say blurred by corporate speak and the language of the marketing brochure?). Are you the same person in this room as you are going to be when they meet you in the coffee break later?

Dimension 3: orientation

Question being asked: Is this person thinking about the issue from my perspective or just from their own?

Focusing on the audience's needs and expectations is not just delivering good customer service, it is an acknowledgement of the fundamental communication principle that says the meaning that the audience assigns to you is the meaning that prevails. We significantly enhance our ability to influence an audience if we not only empathize with their reality, but actually understand it. We reduce our ability to influence if we speak from a selfish stance. Orientation is about answering that pervasive question: "What's in it for me?"

Dimension 4: mechanics

Question being asked: What structures are enhancing or disabling their argument?

The mechanics of your communication encompasses the outer world in which the influence takes place and the "inner world" of the structure and construction of what you are saying. In the outer world, environment matters. If you're doing a presentation, you obviously need to be thinking about the size of the room, the layout of the audience, your command of the stage, your use of visual aids. Are they all in alignment with your material – or does anything get in the way? If you're having a one-to-one talk with someone, environment still matters. Certain venues are appropriate. A chat in the canteen confers informality and friendliness on your words, but is hardly the right context to bring up discipline issues. Other physical environments contain meaning in themselves. To ask someone to "step into my office" may convey powerful meanings which you may or may not intend.

Dimension 5: semantics

Question being asked: Are the words being said compelling and meaningful?

Semantics is to do with the meanings of words. At one end of the scale, this dimension reminds us that to use jargon is OK – as long as all jargon you use is translated into plain English for the benefit of those in the audience who are not familiar with it. (You should note, however, that the use of jargon might be construed by some as arrogance, by others as ignorance.) At the other end of the scale, semantics encourages us to use language that is appropriate to the impact we are trying to have. At times, this could be the plainest of plain speaking. At others, it could be about the vividness of language – a simile, metaphor or story might paint a picture more compelling than a thousand words.

What these five dimensions of influence suggest is that audiences are looking for authenticity – they are looking for you to be yourself – and they are looking for you to speak from their perspective as well as you're own. Both of these are anti-Shadow 3 – which projects an idea of bosses as inhuman (ie lacking any authenticity or human warmth) and selfishness.

What your audience is never looking for when you attempt to persuade them of something are the following:

- A hard sell or a "clever" argument, based on words and word play.

- You to be selfish, short-sighted, unyielding or without compromise.

- The use of political power to force people to be influenced.

Because we are all human – frail, insecure, yielding – we do get influenced by these tactics – especially the latter. But such influence is rarely long lasting, and is never deep. We will always look for ways to get out of a contract we've made with a scum-bucket, even if we know we should never have agreed to sign it in the first place.

Standpoint 2: connecting people to each other

> To create better health in a living system,
> connect it to more of itself.
> Meg Wheatley

Connecting each other 1

Meetings – not necessarily as bad as a poke in the eye with a sharp stick.

Meetings have been given a bad name by business history. Long hours not getting anything done by talking around issues which no one is convinced of the importance of, helping the time to pass by shading in black the spaces created by all the o's and d's on the minutes of the last meeting.

The thing is that we are haunted by what meetings used to be for – telling people stuff they already ought to know. I remember vividly my first ever business meeting. Having welcomed the client, together we all opened up the report our agency had produced. And then my colleague, the project director, began to read it out. Every word.

Today meetings are the very fabric of the knowledge economy and the learning organization. Meetings are not what happens between the work – meetings are the work.

In order to rid ourselves of the weight of history, we need to think and act differently about meetings.

Here are some ways you can signal a change in meetings at your company:

1. Tell people that meetings matter

Meetings are work. Therefore things will need to be achieved in them. Meetings need to produce outcomes. Some of those things we need are in our heads – the knowledge and problem solving abilities we all have. Some of those things can be supplied – an agenda in advance, a room suitable for the meeting's purpose, the necessary technical resources, adequate personal preparation and background research – or created – the right mood or ambience. What we need above all, however, is a commitment to make the meeting work, to help it achieve its outcomes.

So be on time, free yourself mentally from as many other distractions as you can whilst you are in the meeting, turn off the damned mobile phone, and let's get to work.

2. Understand that different outcomes require different methods

A meeting called to generate ideas is going to be different in tone and style to a meeting called to approve the new office design plans. For a start, we won't necessarily need a table in the former; we probably won't need the water pistols, music and bullhorns in the latter. A meeting which needs to make a mission-critical decision will need to have the time and space for silence and reflection – how else will the people therein truly listen to each other, and to their intuition. But a meeting whose objective is to share news and information – and which has a hidden agenda to build community – will probably have more of the noise and energy of a town marketplace.

3. Pay attention to energy flows

No matter how much everyone is committed to being effective in meetings, nevertheless it is hard to stay focused and alert. People are social creatures, but they also are biological, with all manner of chemical gloop running around the body which has us up one minute, and down the next. So feed people well in meetings – water and fruit has got to be better for the human mind–body than another fix of caffeine and sugar. Get people up and moving. Who ever said that thinking and talking were better done sitting down. Take short breaks – with a commitment that people use the breaks to recharge their energy levels, and not to recheck their emails. And if the meeting really isn't working, then be brave enough to call and halt and reschedule rather than drag it on and on beyond everyone's level of effectiveness.

SMART
ANSWERS
TO TOUGH
QUESTIONS

Q: Why does just about every company suffer from apparently "poor communication?"

A: Because they've failed to realize that communication does not just fulfil an intellectual need – the desire to receive and understand information – but an emotional one – the desire to trust and be trusted.

4. Get the information into the meeting room

If someone else outside the meeting has the information the meeting needs, consider calling them up (or better, calling them in) – now. Get that information in the room – it may produce a blip in the meeting flow, but it may also be more effective in the long run than delaying a discussion or decision until "some other time". Such a strategy may minimize individuals' stalling, and reveal resistance to an agenda item more quickly. This strategy should not be used in the place of good preparation (see 1 above).

5. Move from talking to doing

Part of the reason of meeting is social – to be face to face, to share knowledge, to hear and be heard, to make promises, to display ego. But the outcome of the meeting is critical – meeting moves from talking to doing when everyone leaves with a shared understanding of who is responsible for doing what by when. A good meeting has the required technology to create a document that testifies to that shared understanding. Rather than have someone taking notes which later get typed up, get a scribe in with a laptop, projector screen and a printer, so that everyone can see, amend and agree to the "Doing Document" as it is being created. Then they can have the document printed out as the meeting is being wrapped up.

Connecting each other 2

Learning and knowledge management as a day-to-day activity

In chapter 2, we saw how the sources of competitive advantage are seen as moving from the visible to the invisible, from assets and resources (e.g. your buildings, plant and machinery) to knowledge and creativity (what your people know and how they interact to exploit that). In turn this has meant that managers must cease to view organizations as economic entities but social institutions where people are not parts to be replaced or cut but key corporate assets.

Two major disciplines have emerged in the field of management thinking in response to this changing perspective: learning organizations and knowledge management. Each have produced lorry-loads of text and technologies.

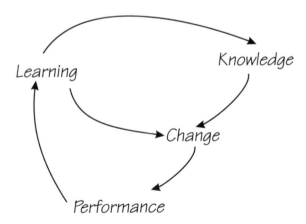

Figure 4.1

The Smart thing to know for the purposes of this chapter is simply that knowledge and learning improve the performance of an organization in a linked and synergistic way (Figure 4.1). (For more on these ideas, see *Smart Things to Know About Knowledge Management*, by Tom M. Koulopoulos and Carl Frappaolo, Capstone.)

So knowledge is power – in the sense that it increases the capacity an individual or organization for effective action.

But organizations have encouraged another interpretation of power – that the power is gained from hoarding knowledge. If I have the knowledge and you don't, I win. Knowledge, this interpretation implies, resides in an individual. Shadow 3 bosses *know*, everyone else *does* . . .

With that dangerous myth prevailing, it has hardly been surprising that learning organization and knowledge management theories have taken longer than common sense would expect to become practical realities. It would have been much easier if we'd have all learnt the reality – that knowledge and learning resides in all of us, that the knowledge and learning of a group is almost always more than the sum of its individual parts, and that hoarding knowledge is a little like trying to hoard oxygen. (The really Smart thing to do with oxygen – if you have some – is to get together with someone who knows how to store it in tanks. With that combination, together we can explore the depths or reach the stars.)

Five roles of a corporate citizen

To realize the true promise of "the knowledge economy", however, we don't necessarily need to understand "knowledge" better. What we

Peter Drucker

Peter Drucker is one of the most revered management thinkers of the last century. His output is all-encompassing as it is prolific, and as Stuart Crainer comments, "There is little that executives do, think or face that he has not written about." He has shown himself to be both prescient and ground-breaking. It was Drucker who introduced the idea of privatization (though the politicians' version of it was less than Drucker's) and it was he who wrote about knowledge workers back in 1969. Drucker understands that a manager is responsible for two equally important facets: (a) "to make human strength effective and human weakness irrelevant" and (b) to be "accountable for results, period". One final thing: he's not keen on you taking early retirement . . .

inevitably need is to expand the roles which people play – or think they play – in organizations as carriers, creators and holders of the knowledge.

Here are five roles you can encourage your team to play to keep the knowledge – and the learning – flowing (source: Nancy M. Dixon, Associate Professor of Administrative Sciences at the George Washington University, Washington DC, USA):

1. Purpose challengers

Purpose challengers ask, in the best possible way, "What's the point?" They actively engage in organizational dialogue that continually examines the worth of the organizations purpose. By bringing discussion of the organizational purpose out into the open, they deliver two benefits. Firstly, they keep the purpose (or vision, or values statement, whatever it might be in your organization) alive. Simply by it being in the conversation means it is not simply a series of words printed in the front of the

Q: Why bother with all this sitting around talking?

Answer 1: It sorts out what's important, what matters, and what is not noise.

> Human nature has never had more information. Paradoxically never has it had less insight into itself. (Rollo May)

Answer 2: Reflection is one of the four pillars of learning. Without it, and with only the other three (question, answer, action) you'll only ever be in headless chicken mode.

Answer 3: Group discussion is a key manifestation knowledge management, simultaneously symbolizing and supplying the worth of participants.

> We don't need more leaders. We need more awareness. (Arnold Mindell)

corporate brochure. And secondly, they allow the purpose to be shaped and adjusted over time, by constructively questioning its relevance to the present.

2. Newscasters

Newscasters ask: "What truth do we need to hear?" Newscasters recognize that part of human nature has a strong tendency to say "nothing's working" or "nothing's changing" or "nothing's happening" or "only awful things are happening – here, let me tell you what they are". Newscasters bring balance to this tendency in people towards the negative and unreal.

Newscasters also "publish – and be damned". In other words, they say what needs to be said. The average employee has their heads full of excuses for staying silent ("You've got to keep your head above the parapet", "They'd never listen anyway", "I've already told them once").

Newscasters cut through all that bullshit and speak up when and where appropriate.

3. Co-creators

Co-creators function as a co-participant in the creation, maintenance and transformation of organizational realities. As we saw in Chapter 1, all people in an organization create the organization. Saying something creates a future of an organization – so does not saying something. Both action and apathy create an organization. For co-creation to work for the greater good, all participants need to believe that what they do can make a difference. That involves not just believing in their own competence; it means trusting that other people will do their bit to change too. There is one more quality that co-creators share: they believe that they have a right to be active participants in their organization. Those who are stuck in a Shadow 3 world where only bosses make things happen can never be true co-creators.

Co-creators also actively participate in the governance of the organization, by expressing their concerns to people who can help those concerns, by asking for information if they feel it is lacking and, most simply, by joining in at meetings, committees, etc.

4. Sharers

People who willingly share what they know for the greater good of the whole are particularly valued. The ability to create a selfish empire based on hoarding of information is an old trick as tired and common as can be and is not required (and should certainly not be rewarded) in a healthy company. This role can only be stepped into when the sense of "we" in the company is stronger than the sense of "I".

Sharers ask 'Who knows what?', 'What knowledge is needed?' and 'What forums and systems will best accelerate knowledge sharing?'

5. Environment scanners

Environment scanning involves keeping abreast of what is happening and changing so that one is an active, responsible, participating citizen of the organization.

In the shorter range, it means "scanning" what's happening now for learning and improvement. A meeting which wraps up with a five minute process review ("How did we do in this meeting?" "What worked well and not so well?", What could we do more effectively next time?") is an example of short-range environment scanning.

How to use the five roles

Share these five roles with your team and you give yourself the chance of:

- Discovering major improvement opportunities – you'll find out what stuff (busyness? bureaucracy? tradition?) gets in the way of people playing the roles.

- Getting to know each other better – our ambitions, values, skills, belief systems in relation to the roles we think we play.

- Analysing frustrations and negative feelings.

- Finding out what else matters most to the team.

> - What are we learning here?
>
> - What's blocking our learning?
>
> - What do we need to unlearn?
>
> Peter Block, in writing about consultants, suggests that they should consider themselves to be "learning architects" – people who build an environment which encourages clients to engage with their problems, learn to adapt and thus move flawlessly into the future. Substitute "clients" for "people" I can think of no better description of the manager in the modern organization.

Smart things to say

Factors that encourage learning in groups

- A love of questions
- Curiosity about what could be better or why things are the way they are now
- A drive for continuous improvement – a continuous dissatisfaction with the status quo

- An external perspective – an eye on the outside world

- Time and a safe space for trial and error – mistakes seen as learning opportunities

- Keeping the creative tension in place between vision and reality

- Compensation or recognition for collective work/communication across boundaries and silos

- Champions and coaches to support learning

- A belief that people *need* to learn

- An understanding that discomfort is a necessary and unavoidable part of the learning experience

Factors that hinder learning

- A desperation for answers

- Complacency, arrogance, over-confidence

- No vision, no understanding of the current reality

- Keeping people separate, keeping them in old divisions, maintaining steady membership of teams

- A lack of time

- A fear of mistakes, condemnation of mistake-makers

- A belief that people ought to *do*

- An understanding that discomfort is a bad thing

- A belief that learning happens only on training courses

If teaching is about giving people the answers, learning must necessarily be about discovering answers yourselves.

But that requires that you must behave as a non-Shadow 3 manager. To create an environment where people learn to adapt to the world and co-create the future, you need to encourage elements of surprise, discovery and "not knowing" into your team. Creating a dependency in your team on your "right answers" (right because you are the boss and not because your answer is appropriate to the need) precludes surprise and discovery and makes smart people stupid. And we will only ever recycle last year's answers, rather than create something ground-breaking and new.

This approach also requires you become comfortable with what is below the surface of your company.

Communication comes from a Latin word meaning to share. What information do we want or need to share in this "communication event"? And how can we make it a "sharing" event – one where everyone has a chance to speak up and co-create the agenda?

Smart things to say

Standpoint 3: connecting people to the deep structure

Regular, meaningful, truly interactive and shared communication does more than keep people informed. It also taps into the deep structure that exists in any group.

Heads up, folks, it's another iceberg (Figure 4.2).

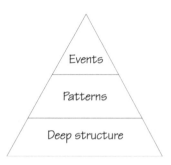

Figure 4.2

Your group creates and talks about events – that's easy because events are observable and, apparently, "true'. Yet, like all icebergs, the danger or potential lurks way beneath the surface. You can try and change events – for example, how people behave towards customers – but unless you work at shifting the deep structure that supports the old behaviour, any new and changed behaviour will drift back to its original state, like a bouy held in place by an anchor on the sea bed. An organization's deep structure, therefore, has a hugely powerful influence over what gets done and how.

In one sense, this model is about human development.

At a low level of organizational development, people just see isolated incidents, occurrences, problems. A problem occurs, and we solve it, because we want to be seen as good and strong and powerful and we want the recognition, acceptance and approval of others that problem solving brings. Time passes, and a similar problem occurs again. And we solve it. Problem, solution, problem, solution. Some people call it firefighting, but I think that's unfair on the noble profession of the firefighter. Because problem, solution, problem, solution simply creates stupid heroes. Heroic because they undoubtedly solve problems. Stupid because they never learn what's causing the problems.

At the level of events, all you can ever do is *react*.

At the next stage of organizational development, human beings create meaning – patterns – out of what happens. They see that these apparently isolated events have in fact got similarities – and some sense can be made out of what before seemed senseless.

Figure 4.3

Here's a small example of what goes on. Your desire for meaning makes you see something in Figure 4.3. What do you see? A box. Actually no, it's just a series of black dots on a white page. You create the box. The box is in your head, based on your past experiences of boxes. Your filter system kicks in to make this potentially senseless string of dots into something meaningful.

The very structure of the human brain seems to press individuals to achieve a sense of completion or closure with respect to perceptions, tasks and activities. . . . It is not surprising then, that the problem of meaningless work is alleviated when workers engage participatively in solving problems and creating changes.

Marshall Shashkin

SMART QUOTES

So too, organizations can learn to see the patterns behind the events. At this level, you can move from simply reacting to *predicting* or *anticipating* events.

The greatest source of power, however, comes from the capacity of an organization – and the people in it – to redesign or transform the deep structure that affects and produces events and patterns.

The deep structure exists not as an organizational chart or the Values and Vision Statement on the wall but as a complex web of largely invisible elements such the following types of (deep) structures:

Formal

- Physical/geographical

- Legal/financial

- Measures of performance/accountability

- Rewards and incentives

- Information flows

- Policies and procedures

Face to face

- Articulated assumptions, beliefs and mental models

Cultural (field)

- Habits and norms

- Shared values in use

- Shared assumptions

- Identity images

(*Source:* adapted from Peter Senge and Bill Isaacs)

In other words, the deep structure exists in our heads, in our conscious or unconscious ideas and beliefs. That's the *cultural* level. It also exists in our language – how we have learnt to speak to each other. That's the *face-to-face* level. And out of those ideas in our heads and words from our mouths, we create the *formal* structures that control what we do.

Deep structure explains why so many organizations are exhausted from change initiatives. It's because people are only trying to shift the formal, visible stuff – a new bonus scheme here, a change of office layout there – without uncovering and recreating the deep structure of beliefs and assumptions which hold things in place. And in time, the deep structure, unchallenged, reasserts itself and pulls all those changed things back towards the status quo. Things make look different on the outside, but in the end its the same old company.

The only way to uncover the deep structure is to observe it in action, or to articulate it in language. Therefore one of the key purposes of communication in organization is not simply to convey information, but to give everyone a regular forum for uncovering the accumulated beliefs, values and assumptions that are subtly informing their behaviour.

Most organizations only think about articulating their deep structure (which might also be called the "corporate culture") when they consciously seek to "change" their culture. They analyse the current culture through audits and surveys, then envision a new, improved culture, and finally work to close the gap. So how often does an organization consider this powerful anchor called deep structure? About once every three years, maybe. Or hardly at all.

The argument here is that organizations and groups can maintain flexibility and power if they remain aware not just of what they want to do, but also aware of the deep structure that supports or restricts their ambitions.

The communicating organization

Here is a template of activities for a communicating organization, that fulfil the need to keep people informed and connected to each other, and to allow you to observe and articulate the deep structure of the group.

How many of these regular communication events could you replicate in your area of responsibility?

Event: start-the-week meetings

Subject: "What's going on?"; news, events, plans, targets

Objective: To give everyone a boost as they begin their week; to give people focus; to share information about ongoing work, partly so that people know what's happening but also to spot any duplication of effort; to connect individual activity to the goals of the team, the department and to the objectives and strategy of the organization; also to make requests of each other for help and support.

Event: end-the-week meetings

Subject: "What happened?"; news, successes, achievements, progress

Objective: To recognize and celebrate accomplishment; to evaluate learning; to chill out, maybe with a beer; to wind down into the weekend; a ritual to mark the transition from worklife to lifelife.

Event: reflections

Subject: What are we experiencing, learning, discovery? What patterns are occurring? Are we creating the place we want to be?

Objective: To spend some time on a regular basis looking at the company from a different perspective, one step removed from the day-to-day detail of the urgent work. This would be a good time to discuss the vision or the values statement: what have we done in the last period of time to move closer to the vision? What's working? What's not?

Event: unit of ones

Subject: Whatever wants to be said.

Objective: To open up a space for anyone who has something to share. Most communication is driven by you the boss. Although most of the time you'll be doing more listening and watching than talking, nevertheless start-the-weeks, end-the-weeks and reflections are all driven by your agenda. What would be communicated if there were no agenda? Create a space in the diary every so often for people to get together to run meetings about whatever is important to them at that time: a skill or piece of knowledge they want to share; a nascent idea they'd like to brainstorm; a provocative business book or article they'd like to debate the merits of.

Event: benchmarking

Subject: What's happening outside of here?

Objective: to learn from and about our competitors. Get a research company in to give you an idea of best practice in your industry. Or if budget forbids, set someone in the team the task of gathering some material from the web. The content they bring to the meeting need not have intellectual rigour of a Gartner Group or a Harvard Business School report – anything that stimulates debate and self-examination in the group is valuable.

Event: customer view

Subject: What are our customers saying about us?

Objective: To listen to what are our customers saying about us? And why? To do ourselves down? So we can get resentful? So that we can pat ourselves on the back. No. So that we can understand regularly that the only arbiter of our quality is the customer's feedback. I learnt this vividly in my time in the theatre. If the audience doesn't believe you're Hamlet, you're not Hamlet, no matter what your ego or the director tells you. The customer view meeting also allows us to shift our perspective from the travails and politics within the organization to the critical challenge of keeping it alive externally in the marketplace.

So, six regular communication events to keep people generating ideas, being reflective and sharing knowledge. Add to all this the regular "normal" meetings you need to have to work together on projects and for problem-solving, and you've maybe got a sense that there are "too many meetings going on around here". When will we get the chance actually to do the "real" work?

But maybe communication is (part of) the real work of an organization. Things change so fast that you need to keep people in touch with those changes (no surprises!) and in touch with their feelings about those changes. Amidst the constant busyness, the neverending activity, there needs to be space for reflection, for sorting out the simply urgent from the urgent and important. And given that communication is a process of people making meaning out of events, you as a manager need to give yourself every opportunity to assert your own intended meaning behind corporate communication – and give yourself every opportunity to keep in touch with unintended meanings that have been produced by the rumour mill and by gossip.

As people mature, a basic human need for autonomy and control over one's own behaviour emerges as part of the natural process of development. While it cannot be suggested that participation in goal setting and decision-making will magically and totally remedy workers" feelings of powerlessness . . . sound evidence indicates that participative management approaches . . . do increase workers' sense of power and control.

Marshall Shashkin

SMART QUOTES

Regular group communications provide you with three major benefits:

- You are giving people every opportunity to talk about activities, successes, priorities, news, victories, failures, learnings. This supplies

KILLER QUESTIONS

Who are we?
and
How do we connect –
to our customers, to
our suppliers, to our
society, to each
other?

information, the message-sending element of communication. It satisfies the human need to know what's going on and to learn.

- It gives people access to power and control: through communication can they make requests of and influence the direction, strategy and purpose.

- At the same time you are giving the group time to listen to how it relates. With regular group interactions you can gauge that "climate" of the team – who is up, who is down, who feels like breaking up. This you can gauge not only by listening to the content of what's said, but by the tones of voice, facial expressions and body language that people use to interact with each other.

- The habitual ways of talking and behaving which are displayed in meetings give you a clue as to the current culture of the group – its deep structure.

The stories that people tell *in* a company are its biggest clues to learning *about* the company.

The spirit-building dimensions of connecting

Communication is far from being an intellectual process alone – although our need to be understood cause us to focus heavily on the *content* of meetings and group interactions. We get the agenda right and then we concentrate on the data, information and knowledge necessary to meet that agenda.

Getting attention

In the September/October 2000 edition of the *Harvard Business Review*, Thomas H. Davenport and John C. Beck underline the necessity of having a central initial in your name. They also have some interesting thoughts on getting the attention you need. They draw some lessons on how to keep your people focused on your company's overarching goals from the "attention industries": the World Wide Web, television, film and print.

The authors argue that the capacity people have for maintaining attention and focusing on the activities that really matter is being eroded by the tidal waves on information that sweep into our lives every day. How many emails and voicemails did you get today?

Since attention is the latest "scare resource", managers need to pay more attention to attention. Lessons are offered for those who want to ensure that their communications get the audience – and the impact – they deserve. The authors' advice, Smart-like, is grounded on their understanding of how people are:

- People are easily scared. Fear grabs the attention. If your communication conveys a threat to security and survival, it is more likely to get heard than one that doesn't (but you won't be able to pull this trick too often).

- People like to compete. Focus people on competitions and measures that show how well they're doing. And what competitor data might motivate them to new heights?

- People are easily distracted. Many companies suffer from "initiative overload". If you launch a new one, either drop an old initiative or two or see if you can mould the new one with some existing initiatives of the same theme and objective. Also note the Ernst and Young Work–Life Balance initiative (and in particular the concierge service) for how some companies formally minimize the impact of non-critical decisions we all have to make.

- People want to connect and engage. Allow them to do that by appealing not just for intellectual acknowledgement, but emotional and psychological commitment too.

Davenport and Beck's research indicates that messages are paid most attention to when they were personalized, evoked an emotional response, were concise and came from a trusted or respected sender.

The manager as facilitator

It used to be that the manager knew all the answers. Now his of her job is to uncover the right questions – and elicit the answers from those who know (and sometimes from those who do not know that they know).

The Institute of Cultural Affairs (ICA) is a global organization dedicated to promote the design and application of methods for human development in communities and organizations. They know – and teach – a lot about partici-pation and facilitation as a management tool.

They suggest the following are the most important elements of a facilitator's style (Source: Laura J. Spenser, *Winning Through Participation*, ICA):

- Relaxed alertness

- Realistic optimism

- Assuming responsibility for the task, the process, the outcome and the participants

- Genuine care for the welfare of the group and the organization

- Honouring the wisdom and creative potential of the group and each individual participant

- Flexibility and responsiveness while keeping the group on track

- Encouraging participation while discouraging individual dominance or side-tracking

- Providing objectivity

- Buffering criticism, anger and frustration to enable the group to progress.

And they have this terrific advice on facilitation techniques:

- The facilitator is an evocateur – someone who elicits answers rather than instructs or imposes them. To do this he or she questions questions ques-tions the group towards shared understanding and consensus.

- The facilitator helps groups achieve objectivity by refraining from judgement and criticism of any idea – but letting the group shape and but into them. He or she also achieves objectivity by focusing on data rather than than each other, thus keeping personalities and personal differences from domi-nating discussion. (This explains why facilitators write so much stuff up on flipcharts or whiteboards – they take the shared focus to the front of the room rather than back to the individual who made the suggestion.)

- A facilitator is a builder of consensus, not a referee in a fight. People are free to criticize and object to anything in a meeting or event – but a constructive principle might be to suggest that no-one is allowed to criticize a statement, idea or suggestion unless they come up with an alternative.

In the Shadow 3 world of hierarchy and political power, all of this is so much malarkey. in the very real world of human beings at work, the concept of manager as facilitator may be one of the key ways to build compelling, healthy and effective organizations.

Communication, however, is also a physical, spiritual and emotional experience.

When you are thinking of bringing people together for a "communication event" of any sort, what considerations are you making for the following:

- Is the physical space conducive to this event? Is the room too big, too small? Does the layout encourage participation? Are there seats for all – or none if you deliberately want people to stand and move about? Does the room itself hold any meaning – positive or negative – that will help or hinder the meeting objectives (compare public space or CEO's office . . .)?

- What breaks are necessary? How will you keep people physically alert and focused?

- Is humour appropriate at this event? What elements of playfulness and celebration will help dissolve tension, mark transition or create a feeling of unity and human warmth?

- What could be on the walls?

- What refreshments are appropriate? Beer, wine and soft drinks on a Friday afternoon debrief perhaps? A gift of a doughnut for each participant at a more intimate meeting might in a small way set a tone of graciousness and thoughtfulness.

- Is music necessary to signal a break, or to provide a subtle background for brainstorming? When and how can you inject silence for personal reflection into a noisy meeting?

The derivation of the word culture is centred in the concept of reverential homage. Every culture has its roots in a myth that allows members to explain why life is the way it is. The shared belief that this myth is real is the "gel" of culture. This is the myth of why we do the things we do.

Watts Wacker

Organizations are conversations

In one sense, the quality of an organization's outputs – its products, services, its actions and results, its success in the external world – is a reflection of the quality of its internal relationships – its ability to connect people together and exploit their knowledge and talents for the good of the whole. The only way people are connected together is through their ability to communicate with each other.

Anita Roddick

Anita Roddick founded The Body Shop in 1976 in Brighton, England with £12,000 to her credit. She was a 33-year-old housewife who opened a store to support herself and her two children while her husband pursued a lifelong passion to ride a horse from Brazil to New York (men!). The company has grown to 1,700 stores in 49 countries selling environmentally friendly beauty products but Roddick is known as much for her ethical and moral campaigning as her business acumen. In 1998 she stepped down from the chief executive position as part of a fundamental shake-up of the company. She still shares the role of co-chairman with her husband (now back from his trip) though Roddick has indicated that she is going to quit the daily work of the business to campaign for human rights. Love her or hate her, Anita Roddick's stance is one that shows that it is possible to maintain the highest ethical standards in a competitive and capitalistic society.

"Really, it's really easy. There's a terrorism of language that says you either have to do this or that. I like to call it the genius of the End. You can be ethical, you can be honest and you can be transparent. You can keep your shareholders happy and you can be a company that is more about public good than private greed. You can say no to sweatshops and to child labour and find more honourable ways of trading. Sometimes, you just have to say 'up your bum' to those institutions that say to maximize profits. My duty is to keep this company alive, not just to maximize profits. That could turn me into a criminal."

Everything you do, Anita Roddick reminds us, is an outward symbol of who you are and what you stand for (which is why she calls he stores "arenas of education").

In one sense, then, an organization is a product of conversation. As a manager, one of your jobs is to ensure that the conversations you are part of are as effective possible.

But what are the attributes of healthy, effective conversations which you need to practice?

First, as the fifth discipline and learning organization work of Peter Senge *et al.* has made clear, we need to remember that conversations are a balance between advocacy (telling, explaining) and enquiry (asking, seeking).

So strongly is our business communication culture grounded in the need to control others – to present facts and arguments, to persuade others that we are right or worthy of respect, to convince and influence – that we have almost lost the understanding that conversation is a two-sided, co-creative medium. There are clearly times when it is absolutely appropriate that a manager tells his people what to do, and concentrates on advocacy over enquiry. But participative approaches to teambuilding, problem solving and knowledge sharing demands that we try to let go of the need to "win" in a conversation. True conversation is creative and synergistic – it creates something that was not there before, and often something beyond the initial ambitions of the separate participants.

One thing you might ask yourself, therefore, before engaging someone in conversation is how open you are to being influenced. Or is your position utterly fixed?

Balancing advocacy and enquiry

Being a strong advocate means clearly stating your opinions, ideas and suggestions and revealing the reasoning, assumptions and thinking that went on in creating those assertions ("This is what I suggest and this is why I say it . . ."). Like an iceberg, much of human communication is invisible and goes on in the depths of our minds, prior to and whilst the words are being said.

Shadow 3 managers hide their reasoning, seeing it as a weakness. How vulnerable they would be if their reasoning was shown to be faulty! Smart managers who value the participation of their people see revealing their reasoning as an opportunity for feedback and a way of allowing others to build on the thinking and taking it into new and possibly better areas.

Being a strong advocate also means seeking to engage the other person – constantly checking that the person is really listening and inquiring regularly as to their reactions and thoughts.

Finally, strong advocacy, even though it is about telling someone something, is nevertheless grounded in listening. Listening for reaction – so that the telling can be shaped to suit the situation – and listening for silence or doubt that would indicate confusion or antipathy.

Enquiry, pretty obviously, proactively seeks information from the advocate or teller ("Tell me more, tell me about how you came to that view"). But good enquirers also explain why they asking the question – signalling their own thinking and reactions and intentions.

In this way, healthy conversation is truly about revealing the thinking that goes on behind talking, and therefore minimizes the paranoia and pain that results from misunderstanding, assumed intentions and judgement.

Two final important questions:

1. Has this conversation produced a change? Does this conversation lead to an action or action plan? What would signal a visible result from this exchange?

2. Do all participants in this conversation feel satisfied? Do they feel listened to and understood? Have they reached completion on this matter, or is anything outstanding or unsurfaced (practically or emotionally)?

Smart things to remember

Protocols for generative conversations

Here is what I think and how I got there.

Do you see any gaps in what I just said?

Do you see it differently?

What leads you to conclude that . . . XYZ?

I am asking because . . . ABC?

What do we do to move forward?

At moments of conflict:
When you said/did (insert *data*), I felt (insert *emotion*), because I made an interpretation or assumption that (insert *inference*); and what I would like is (insert *request*).

(*Source*: Alain Gauthier, Ursula Versteegen, Organizational Learning Workshop)

Communication is a human process, but increasingly – for better or worse – carried out through technology, and in particular, by email. I know some people who email their colleagues two desks away rather than face them in the flesh. I know many people who boast (under the guise of complaining about it) about the number of emails they have to deal with on their return from vacation. (Before email, people would boast about the length of their To-Do list. Before To-Do lists, they'd satisfy the same urge for competition and ego by sneaking a look at each other in the shower after a game of squash.)

Since email is such an ubiquitous medium, and one, like all human inventions, blessed and plagued with both promise and threat, I asked Bob Helliwell of Team IT Training (who claim to save their clients 30 minutes per person per day on email use!) to give us all some advice on this powerful medium.

Smart Things to Know About Email

Principles

Here are some key principles for communicating by email:

- The meaning of your communication is the response you elicit.
- You are a part of the system which is producing the email traffic you are receiving. If you send out lots of copies of email, you will receive lots of copies.
- If you receive irrelevant messages and you do nothing, you will continue to receive them.
- If you are dissatisfied with your email traffic (quality, quantity, frequency) and you do nothing about it Ð then nothing will change.

You only have words

In face-to-face communication, you convey meaning with:

- the words you choose
- how you say those words
- your facial expression
- your other body language.

On the telephone, you can only get your message across with:

- the words you choose
- how you say them.

With email you only have:

- the words

So if there is a strong emotional content to your message and you are sending an email, either you get your message across with just the words or you do not get it across at all.

You cannot not communicate

- Even if you do not send a reply to an email, that sends a message: perhaps a tacit acceptance that it is OK to send you that type of mail.

Smart assumptions not to make

- I've sent it, so it has arrived. (They might be off line.)

- It has been opened, so it's been read. (They may have just previewed the email – possibly by accident.)

- It's a private and secure medium. (It might be read by your systems people, theirs or anyone else who walked past their desk.)

- Email is transient. (It will exist on a backup somewhere almost indefinitely.)

SMART emailers lead by example.

- They send clear, well laid-out and easily read emails which are relevant to the recipient.

- They are proactive in eliciting the type of email traffic they want.

- They elicit feedback from their colleagues about the emails they have sent

- They let their colleagues know their response times: how often they check their mail, if it is better to contact them by telephone at certain times.

Relationships and email

There are broadly three categories of people you communicate with by email: those you know well, those you know slightly and those who are complete strangers.

Email is a generally informal medium: "Hi there", is an acceptable beginning to a business email, but not a business letter.

Be careful to match your (in)formality to the reality of your email relationship: the less well you know someone, the more you should verge on the formal.

Meta messages

Watch out for meta messages which can send a whole other layer of meaning:

- Copying in someone's boss sends an extra message about (lack of) trust.

- Copying the whole organization sends a message about how you value their time.

- Sending a poorly spelled email sends a message about your attention to detail.

Subject lines

- Set the reader up to read your message.

- What will be the best subject line to give them an idea of what is in the message and to help them prioritize?

- Don't make it too long (it might get truncated) and never leave it blank.

Attachments

Be particularly considerate to people who need to dial in to collect their mail. They will not thank you for sending them large, irrelevant attachments.

If sending attachments to a group, consider using a bulletin board or intranet – and sending the group an address where they should look.

Copying: quality versus quantity

On the one hand, it's good to keep your staff up to date on what is happening, but do they really need all that information?

Out of courtesy, a local authority manager was routinely copying in her staff on all the information she was getting from her boss about their directorate.

Finally one of her staff cracked. He printed out everything she sent him for a month and at their monthly meeting, he showed her two filing boxes stuffed to overflowing with every document she had copied him in on.

Until she actually saw the volume, she had not realized how much she was overloading her staff. She would never have expected someone to keep up to date with that amount of paper-based material.

She now thinks more carefully about why she is forwarding material to her staff.

How much of your reply is relevant?

When replying to a group email, does everyone need the same email or should you segment your audience and send separate ones?

Instead of adopting the standard way email packages set you up to reply (all old text at the bottom, your new text at the top) – try this instead:

- strip out all irrelevant text
- write "you said" to indicate their original message
- intersperse your answer within their text so they start reading at the top of the message and continue smoothly through.

Anger

Don't reply to an angry email with another email. Use a medium of communication with instantaneous feedback – either meet them face-to-face or use the telephone.

Stories

Here are two stories that summarize what we're on about here:

1. How not to say "Good morning"

Because you don't see the reaction your email provokes does not mean it has not provoked one.

The team worked in an open-plan office.

Every morning their manager would walk through the middle of them, not making eye contact. He would go into his office, close the door and power up his computer. Then he routinely sent an email to the team saying "Good morning, everybody. I'm in now."

Granted, he did not see the reactions he provoked every morning. Nevertheless those reactions happened – in all his staff, every day.

How many ways is this an inappropriate use of the medium of email?

2. Three words that demotivated a team

When you write an email, you may have a particular tone of voice in your head. When someone reads it they will not have the same one in theirs.

A manager of a 20-person team in an international telecommunications company had just heard the results of the team's salary review. Part of the team was away, returning in two days time. The manager himself needed to go abroad for two days and his absence overlapped theirs.

As he wanted to give everyone the results of the salary review at the same time, he sent a "holding" email to the whole team informing them when he would pass on the results.

He knew the results were all favourable, so he was in a good mood as he wrote this email:

"I've had the results from the salary review. I am away till Friday so I will give you the good (or the bad!) news on my return."

When he wrote "or the bad!" he was chuckling as he pulled their legs. When they read it, however, they were outraged at the possibility of a salary cut.

The whole team was demotivated by those three words and spent most of the time until his return grumbling by the kettle.

Email is the fastest-growing means of communication and so far traffic is doubling every two years. Smart people will put these points into practice and manage their email. Others will let their email manage them.

        Bob Hallewell, Director of Team IT Training, bobh@teamittraining.com

5

Achieving

This chapter examines how you get things done in the modern organization and re-evaluates some traditional management tools in the light of a changed and changing working environment.

There are three channels to getting things done through people. Each of them operates from the principle that people need to be seen as strong or good, and that they need constant reaffirmation and recognition to make them feel that.

Here are the three channels:

1. Reaffirm people's sense of identity and possibility

How? Do this through an understanding of

- Motivation

- Objective-setting

2. Help them inspire themselves

How? Do this through an application of these practices

- Coaching

- Delegation

- Rewards

- Celebration

3. Minimize confusion and paranoia

How? Do this through the tools of

- Feedback

- Performance appraisals

In this chapter, we'll look at these channels one at a time.

Making things happen 1: reaffirm people's sense of identity and possibility

Motivation

Motivation is a force people generate which compels them to act. Motivation is fuelled by the answers to three questions:

- Am I worthy of success?

- Am I capable?

- Am I pulled towards the future by a goal/vision/ambition?

Smart things to say

Things work out best for those who make the best out of the way things work out

In other words, a motivated person is one who has a strong sense of confidence in themselves and a powerful attraction to some future state. These are issues of identity and possibility. Both are needed for people to succeed.

People can only ever motivate themselves – and are constantly doing so. The trouble is that the level or direction of their motivation may not be what is required by you or the organization. To paraphrase Arnold Mindell, we don't need more motivational speakers, we need more self-awareness. Why? Because people are always motivating themselves based on what they think they need to do to survive.

Actors want to know "what's my motivation?" The truth of life is that most of us have no idea about our motivations . . .

(with thanks to Will Self)

SMART QUOTES

Survival is the bottom line. The world of business with all its macho overtones and love affair with sports analogies likes to talk about playing to win or being a winner. A Smart Thing to Know about People is to remember that the vast majority of people aren't even in the game to win. Most people are following their conditioning *not to lose* . . .

So the Smart motivator would spend less time painting wonderful dreams of the future and telling inspirational stories of ordinary people overcoming extraordinary odds. These tales, full of sound and fury, undoubtedly work in that they affect the imagination. People can dream, people like to be excited. But the effect is only temporary. When the adrenaline has stopped pumping, everyone realizes that the "vision", however attractive, has not changed anything in the present.

So the Smart motivator spends less time on that and more time helping people identify and remove the self-imposed habits and stories they create which only ever allow them *not to lose* . . .

SMART QUOTES

Human life will never be understood unless its highest aspirations are taken into account. Growth, self-actualization, the striving toward health, the quest for identity and autonomy, the yearning for excellence (and other ways of phrasing the striving "upward") must by now be accepted beyond question as a widespread and perhaps universal human tendency. And yet there are also other regressive, fearful, self-diminishing tendencies as well, and it is very easy to forget them in our intoxication with "personal growth," especially for inexperienced youngsters. . . . We must appreciate that many people choose the worse rather than the better, that growth is often a painful process . . .

Abraham Maslow, *Motivation and Personality*

The most common habits people have in the *playing not to lose* survival game are these:

Blame

The easiest place to be is in the place of blame, because whatever is wrong is always someone else's fault. Don't let people linger there. Life is not about what happens to you but how you respond to what happens to you.

How to tackle blame: Push people into their circle of responsibility – encourage them to think only about what they themselves can influence or change about the situation.

Inflexibility of perception

Life is a complex undertaking, full of unpredictability and complication. People know this, particularly with regard to their personal life. But when they get into an organization, they somehow expect things to be different. They expect their bosses to be able to know everything, act impeccably and guarantee the future – and expect to be able to criticize when him or her when they fail to live up to this ridiculous expectation. In other words, people lose the ability to be flexible, to see things from more than one perspective. The way they see the problem, they assert, is the right way.

How to tackle inflexibility of perception: Encourage your people to consider all perspectives on a situation – "What are we not considering here?" "Who would see this differently and what can we learn from that?"

Fearfulness

Fear is a mental creation people project onto a situation in order to justify them not taking a risk. Fear might not be a great thing to feel, but at least it justifies not risking survival.

How to tackle fearfulness: The Smart coach and manager plays two roles simultaneously when faced with a fearful employee. First you must be empathetic – you must listen intently, feel and show concern. People sometimes need a shoulder to cry on and they need to see or hear the equivalent of the phrase: "Oh I know, it's just awful." But you can't leave or keep people there in the place of empathy – they might never get out of it. You must now shift to playing change agent:

> "OK, what do you have control over?"
> "OK, what action can you take?"
> "OK what can you do anyway, even though you're afraid?"

Solemnity

Solemnity is a mask people use to demonstrate how clever and disciplined they are. Or they use solemnity to attempt to demonstrate that their situation is so serious and difficult, that no solution you could offer is going to work. (Playing to lose is the ego's way of surviving – it tells you that it might be threatened if it's perceived as foolish or silly.)

How to tackle solemnity: Take the person out of their current situation. Literally change their state by changing the place you're in (physical movement tends to shift people out of emotional stagnation – breathing helps too). Solemn people tend to be too stiff to breath well.

Our worst fear is not that we are inadequate, our deepest fear is that we are powerful beyond measure. It is our light, not our darkness that most frightens us. We ask ourselves,"Who am I to be brilliant, gorgeous, talented and fabulous?" Actually, who are you not to be? You are a child of God; your playing small doesn't serve the world. There is nothing enlightening about shrinking so that other people won't feel insecure around you. . . . As we are liberated from our own fear our presence automatically liberates others.

Marianne Williamson

Abraham Maslow

Abraham Maslow (1908–1970) was, from 1937 to 1951, on the faculty of Brooklyn College. There he was mentored by the anthropologist Ruth Benedict and the Gestalt psychologist Max Wertheimer. Maslow so admired their professional achievements and personal attributes that he began to study what it was that made them so successful as human beings. His work in mental health and human potential was at odds with the study of psychology to date, which had focused largely on what was wrong with people who were mentally ill.

Maslow is most remembered for his concept of the "hierarchy of needs".

Maslow saw human beings' needs arranged like a pyramid or ladder. The most basic needs, at the bottom, were *physiological needs* – food, water, oxygen and sex. The concept suggests that as one set of needs is met, the person moves up the ladder to the next. In Maslow's concept, *safety needs* are next: security, stability, dependency, protection, freedom from fear, anxiety and chaos, need for structure, order, law, and limits, and strength in the protector. It is interesting to reflect on how far organizations play on and exploit this relatively low-level human need . . .

Belongingness and love needs are next, and here we find the need for the recognition, acceptance and approval of others.

Esteem needs too require us to have a stable, firmly based, usually high evaluation of ourselves, for self-respect or self-esteem, and for the esteem of others.

At the top of the ladder are what Maslow terms *self-actualizing needs* – the need to fulfil oneself, to become all that one is capable of becoming:

> Musicians must make music, artists must paint, poets must write if they are to be ultimately at peace with themselves. What humans can be, they must be. They must be true to their own nature. This need we may call self-actualization.

Self-actualizing people, he suggests, tend to focus on problems outside of themselves, have a clear sense of what is true and what is sham, are spontaneous and creative, and are not bound too strictly by social conventions. Maslow later redefined self-actualization as a function of frequency of peak experiences – profound moments of love, understanding, happiness or rapture, when a person feels more whole, alive, self-sufficient and yet a part of the world and more aware of such high values as truth, justice, harmony and goodness.

Playing small

The sub-game of "playing small" is present when you hear people saying:

- I couldn't possibly because I'm only . . .
- It's not my job, you know . . .
- Someone else ought to do something . . .

How to tackle playing small: By being intolerant of it. Playing small is an offence to the person's own sense of self-worth (although they may have craftily reduced their self-worth to match their expectations in life). It should certainly be offensive to you, who has to every month sign off this person's salary cheque. Did you realize that you were going to be paying good money to a person who's shrunk themselves so much since the interview process?

Giving people what they want

People are desperate for acceptance, approval and recognition. It may be pathetic but it's true (true for you and me both). So give it to them:

- Praise people often so that people see it as part of your personality and style. People will find it easier to get what they want (acceptance, approval and recognition) knowing that you are a chronic praiser, as long, of course, they give you what you want (achievement of performance goals).

- Praise publicly and privately, depending on what would have biggest impact on all concerned (but always criticize in private unless, of course, it is the group which needs criticizing).

- Praise what is good for the greater good (e.g. praise instances of effective collaboration if teamwork is an organizational value)

- Praise effort and hard work towards achievement as well as achievement towards the end goals. Some projects are so complex and long that to leave compliments until the end of it would leave people *praise-starved*

- Praise but don't patronize . . .

Keep in mind the sharp distinction between acknowledgement and praise. The latter – with its gold-star, grade-school roots – is extrinsic and patronizing. It can fuel internal competition. It's a manifestation of our worst top-down inclinations. Acknowledgement, on the other hand, is grounded in respect and gratitude. It knows that people do great work because of deep interests, passions, commitment – stuff that comes from within.

Tom Terez

- Praise because you want to, not because you feel you ought to. The trouble is you really ought to praise, and probably more often than
  – you want to
  – you think you already do
  – you have the time to

So if you find yourself with nothing to praise, you need to look at yourself first. You need to reassess your purpose and roles as a manager and look at how you manage your time. If there's nothing to praise, what on earth have you been doing? And if there's really nothing going on that's worthy of praise, then you need to take responsibility for what you've helped to produce . . . and get coaching...

Making things happen 2: help them to inspire themselves

The art of great management is to provide an environment – and as part of that, a series of relationships and interactions – which allow people to set their own high standards of success. Proactive, creative people do not appear to need others to make them aim high – they appear to inspire themselves.

Three motivation gurus (theory variety)

Frederick Herzberg

Frederick Herzberg's two-factor theory overturned traditional thinking about job satisfaction which assumed that one could either be satisfied, dissatisfied or somewhere along a spectrum linking the two. In fact, asserted Herzberg, a worker could move between satisfied and dissatisfied on certain motivation factors (such as achievement, recognition, responsibility and advancement) and from dissatisfied to no dissatisfaction on certain hygiene factors (such as working conditions, relations with the boss and collegues, pay and company policies). The two-factor theory suggests that a manager must make sure that a job's hygiene factors are in no way deficient (so fair pay, safe conditons, etc.) and then proceed to give employees experience of as many motivation factors as possible.

David C. McClelland

David C. McClelland is associated with human need theory, which asserts that people have urges (variously) towards three needs: the need for achievement (the desire to accomplish a goal more effectively than in the past): the need for affiliation (the desire for human companionship and acceptance) and the need for power (the desire to be influential in a group and to control one's environment). Studies indicate that successful managers have stronger power motives than less successful managers – so get the whip ready and practice curling your lip.

Victor Vroom

Victor Vroom (not a Marvel comics character) developed the framework for expectancy theory, which asserts that people make choices from alternative possibilities of action based on how much they want a thing and how likely they think they are to get it.

Perhaps the single biggest truth out of these theorists is that high performance in a job leads to high satisfaction for it, and not the other way round. This underlines the need for Smart managers to treat each employee as an individual and to act as a coach who brings out the best in them. People moving towards greatness (whatever that is for each individual) is what cultivates great places to work.

But what helps them achieve that level of excellence is a great coach.

Coaching

Coaching is a process and style of interaction which moves people to improve their performance by tapping in to their own innate power and competence.

Training and mentoring give people the skills and perspectives they need to achieve their goals and which are probably currently missing. So training and mentoring are often complementary development skills to the coaching process – part of the process might identify skills that are absent for example.

The coaching process has six stages:

1. Sets goals or performance levels.

2. Finds out what is missing which if present would make this goal achievable.

3. Explores why what is missing is missing.

4. Identifies a plan of action that moves the person closer to the goal.

5. Maintains contact with the person over time to monitor progress – giving support, guidance or motivation as required

6. Celebrates the successful achievement of the goal

What makes a successful coach?

Another motivation guru (stage variety)

"Who is Anthony Robbins?" asks the website dedicated to him: www.tree-seminars.com. And it answers it as if the concept understatement had not been invented:

Anthony Robbins is a creative genius. . . . Many years of commitment to learning, growing, and contributing to improving the quality of life for people worldwide has earned Anthony Robbins the unmatched reputation as the leader in the personal and professional improvement industry. Anthony Robbins has become a brand name as America's peak performance coach, a world communicator and cutting-edge turnaround expert.

Whatever it is he does, he gets results. More than 1 million people have attended Anthony Robbins' live seminars, from 42 nations around the world; he has sold more than 3 million copies of his books (*Unlimited Power* and *Awaken the Giant Within*); sold more than 24 million educational tapes; consults to prominent world figures for a fee of $1 million per year; and currently commands $160,000 per speaking engagement and a consulting fee of $1–4 million annually for business leaders.

Anthony Robbins has been a private coach to Bill Clinton, Andre Agassi, Mikhail Gorbachev and Pamela Anderson. Which is a combination to make the mind boggle . . .

A great coach is someone who:

- is passionate about seeing people successfully achieve goals – a coach's personal fulfilment is almost vicarious, coming through others" success. Coaching is a work of service to others. Egos are not required.

- is able to inspire people to see goals as important, rewarding and worthy of hard work.

- has relationship style width; is soft enough to be empathetic about the pressures that create the current level of performance and also hard enough to outline that level as unacceptable to all concerned (organization, coach and coached). In America they call this tough love.

- has performance style width; can be directive towards those who are unsure of what to do and facilitative towards those are more confident.

- can build a bond of trust quickly.

- can provide honest feedback effectively – can give hard messages in a way that aids rather than cripples the person being coached.

- has the credibility that only past coaching success can bring.

- is generous and flexible – does everything required when it's required to allow the person to achieve (include being there, sharing knowledge, being positive in the face of negativity, remaining calm in the face of stress).

- is perceptive: listens for clues behind the words spoken that will provide the (psychological) evidence as to why current levels of success are the way they are. In other words can identify habits of thinking, talking and acting which are not helpful to the goal

Why is coaching such an effective way of managing? There are three answers:

1. It clarifies and improves performance – and performance is what

Setting SMART objectives

We need to understand exactly what we have to do to add value to the organization within each of our major responsibility areas. These are our objectives.

We also need to understand all of the "boundary conditions" that are either enablers or constraints on our "freedom" to act.

S Specific, Stretching, Supported, Success-orientated

M Measurable, Minimum Acceptable

A Achievable, Agreed, Action-orientated

R Realistic, Required Resources, Reviewable

T Time-Bounded, Trackable

Rationale

1. We need to be specific and action-orientated in defining what we intend to achieve.

2. We need to define measures that we can use to track and review progress and demonstrate success.

3. We also need to know what is the minimum acceptable level of achievement whilst aiming for greater success.

4. We need to clarify which resources are required and available.

5. We need to agree the support we need from our line manager.

6. We need to negotiate what is realistic, achievable and stretching.

7. Having agreed the objective, we need to commit to delivering it within the expected time scale.

8. We need to write down our objectives in a SMART way.

from George Oakham, The Facilitated Workshop Workbook
(Centre for Effective Business Development Ltd.)

makes organizations tick. Coaching links individual goals to organizational objectives.

2. It focuses on and works with the individual. The coachee might say when the achieved goal is being celebrated "Hey Coach, I couldn't have done it without you!" But the converse is undeniably true. A coach asks good questions – the right questions at the right time – but the answers always eventually come from the coachee

3. Coaching is a creative act: it creates something that was not there before the coaching began. That might be the all important achieved goal, of course – but consider the long list of other things created which are equally valuable both to the individual and the organization:

- Enhanced self-esteem

- Insight into own habits and foibles

- Learning of new competence

- Development of current competence

- Focus and discipline

- Confidence to take on new and bigger goals

SMART QUOTES

Perhaps the most valuable result of all education is the ability to make yourself do the thing you have to do when it ought to be done whether you like it or not. It is the first lesson that ought to be learned and however early a person's training begins, it is probably the last lesson a person learns thoroughly.

Thomas Huxley

Delegation

Delegation is what allows your organization to happen. Why? Because you really can't do it all yourself. And even if you're one of those sad people whose mother convinced them that you really can all do it yourself, you'd still fail as a manager because not delegating consigns your people to be bitter or disillusioned or lazy or complacent – and it certainly means that they'll never grow or develop their competence for that time when you do want them to do something.

So delegation

- Divides up complex and multiple projects

- Clarifies goals and standards

- Assigns responsibility and prevents duplication of effort

- Develops experience, competence and confidence

- Pushes the organization into the future

The two big barriers to delegation are:

1. The lure of the Third Quadrant (see panel on Stephen Covey)
   You think it's quicker to do something yourself.
   The danger here is that you're consigned to forever having to do it, long after you've finally seen the error of your ways and have stopped wanting to do it.

2. Your ego
   You think no one else can do it as well as you

The danger here is that you reinforce the situation over time, maybe

Stephen R. Covey

Stephen Covey, who bills himself first in his public biogs as husband, father and grandfather, is also one of the most successful management gurus of the 20th century. Quite apart from selling shiploads of *The Seven Habits of Highly Effective People* books, tapes and seminars, and creating the Covey Leadership Center to maximize the opportunities coming out of such sales, Covey found himself called on by the Bill Clinton administration (along with Anthony Robbins).

His *First Things First* (written with A. Roger and Rebecca R. Merrill) is by far his most practical book, centring as it does on the way people use or abuse the one resource which once spent is gone forever: time.

I can recommend the book in full, but here is an abstract of some key ideas which you can start using for your own self-organization today. Central to this work is that it is about your life — and what gives it importance and purpose — as much as the efficiency of your business. The business world, suggests Covey, has produced too many suicidal, depressed, addicted, divorced but extremely efficient people.

Activities tend to fall into one of four categories or Quadrants:

Quadrant 1 Urgent and important

Crises

Pressing problems

Deadline-driven meetings, projects, preparations

Quadrant 2 Important but not urgent

Preparation

Prevention

Planning

Relationship building

Seizing new opportunities

Personal development of self and others

Quadrant 3 Urgent but not important

Interruptions, some phone calls

Some mail

Some reports, meetings

Many proximate matters

Quadrant 4 Not urgent and not important

Trivia

Busywork

Some phone calls

Time wasters

"Escape" activities

The energy of urgency, says Covey, often convinces us to think that those things which are not important are so, and thus too much time is lost in Quadrant 3 activities. The macho, activity-driven world of business may also produce more urgency-addicts than is healthy.

How to plan your week the Covey/Merrill way

1. Connect to what's most important to you in your life as a whole: what do you want to do and be in life?

2. Identify the many roles you play in your work and life – board member, wife, PTA member – as well as the distinct roles you play in each area. (Being a manager, for example, splits down into manager as coach, manager as leader, manager as administrator, etc., and each of these things places demands on your time.)

3. Select a weekly goal for each role: what is the most important thing I could do in this role this week to have the greatest positive impact.

4. Begin to prioritize your time, putting the important things (Quadrant 2 activities; weekly goals) in the diary or planner first (on the principle that if you put those in first, anything else you have to do will fit around it, but if

you let the other things eat up your time, then you may struggle to find time for those important but not urgent tasks).

5. Some priorities are time-sensitive — they have a specific time to be achieved at or in. Other urgent and important tasks, of course, crop up which we could not have anticipated at the beginning of the week. Other priorities (e.g. "Spend time with my family") need you to look for an opportunity to do them. Writing your priorities/goals/Quadrant 2 activities down, and carrying them over from day to next day if you fail to meet them, keeps them top of mind, rather than bottom of the list.

6. Evaluate your week as it ends: reflect on what you achieved against what you intended to achieve, what obstacles you faced and what you can learn towards being more effective next time.

unconsciously. You make sure that you create that which you most don't want. After all, you don't want to prove yourself wrong. So you produce people who "don't have all the information they need to do this job" by not giving them the information. You produce people who make mistakes, because you give them information but no context. And so on.

A delegation checklist

So what are the key stages of delegation? If we were to write it as a checklist, it would look something like this:

☐ Explain why the job is important – be specific and clear – and its priority against other current tasks.

☐ Clarify the results you expect. Explain why you have chosen this person to do the task, and the qualities they have that will help them achieve it.

- [ ] How will the person you are delegating to know that the task has been achieved?
- [ ] Define the authority level:
    - [ ] Level 6: "Take action – no further contact with me is required."
    - [ ] Level 5: "Take action – let me know what you did."
    - [ ] Level 4: "Look into it – let me know what you intend to do; do it unless I say no."
    - [ ] Level 3: "Look into it – let me know what you intend to do; don't take action unless I approve."
    - [ ] Level 2: "Look into it – let me know possible actions, including pros and cons of each, and recommend one for my approval."
    - [ ] Level 1: "Look into it – report all the facts to me: I'll decide what to do."
- [ ] Agree on a deadline
- [ ] Obtain feedback. Check understanding of the task and the degree of commitment to it.
    - [ ] If there is some resistance to the task, name it and talk about it. Focus on the concerns of the person concerned, and tackle each separately. Focus too on the need for success, not possible reasons for failure.
- [ ] Provide for controls – interim review points relevant to the authority level.

Follow up is critical. Although it is a delegated job, only a level 6 delegation absolves you of the responsibility for knowing exactly what the

Jack Welch

Since Jack Welch assumed the position of CEO at General Electric in 1981, the company has soared to the top of the Fortune 500, with a market capitalization in excess of $250 billion. It is, in fact, the most valuable company in the world and he is one of the most respected business leaders and today.

What does he believe? For the answer to that question, just have a look at the chapter headings of his book *Jack Welch and the GE Way: Management Insights and Leadership Secrets of the Legendary CEO* by Robert Slater:

Jack Welch Launches His Revolution

Part I   Act Like a Leader, Not a Manager

1   Embrace Change, Don't Fear It

2   Stop Managing, Start Leading

3   Cultivate Managers Who Share Your Vision

4   Face Reality, Then Act Decisively

5   Be Simple, Be Consistent, and Hammer Your Message Home

Part II   Building the Market-leading Company

6   Be Number 1 or Number 2, But Don't Narrow Your Market

7   Look for the Quantum Leap!

8   Fix, Close, or Sell: Reviving NBC

9   Don't Focus on the Numbers

10 Plagiarize – It's Legitimate: Create a Learning Culture

Part III   Forging the Boundaryless Organization

11 Get Rid of the Managers, Get Rid of the Bureaucracy

12 Be Lean and Agile Like a Small Company

13 Tear Down the Boundaries

Part IV   Harnessing Your People for Competitive Advantage

14 Three Secrets: Speed, Simplicity, and Self-Confidence

15 Use the Brains of Every Worker – Involve Everyone

In other words, he's a shy retiring type who you'd barely notice if he walked through the door. Maybe.

outcome was, and no level suggests that you are free of responsibility for its quality being achieved. (Other people, elsewhere in the organization, who are affected by the delegated task may well have very strong feelings about whether that task is still your responsibility or that of the person it was delegated to.)

So, organize yourself to keep a record of your people's performance goals and measures and keep track of the key review points.

And the smart phrase to use when at those review points is not:

"Tell me, how's it going?" but "Please, show me how it's going!"

Celebration and fun

A great coach is someone who provides constant encouragement and praise – even through the bad days, there's a voice there for people who have begun to doubt they can succeed.

In business, there is a tendency to use celebration as a reward – a little party here, a couple of tinnies there, maybe a few words from the boss; a balloon – to mark the successful completion of a project. It's a cause and effect sort of thing.

The problem with this approach is that it puts off until tomorrow what we could have today. And in a world of increasing speed and complexity, the danger is that tomorrow never comes. How many projects do you know where all the personnel who kicked it off are still in place

Q: What's the point all this "fun at work" we hear so much about?

A: Ah, just a few short years ago, you'd have been scoffed at for even suggesting the concept. But times are changing:

> Like art, play is going through an equally as provocative redefinition of its essence. Play organized around chaos suggests that we will be playing at times when we used to never consider it. Is that not what is driving the agenda of work? We have learned that when people are playing, they are at their most creative and they are also in their most receptive environment to learning. Like never before, people are being encouraged to play and to be playful while they are at work. People are beginning to fuse their work and their "play" environments such that there is blurring of the boundaries to the maximum extent possible.

> The final issue for thought is celebration. When we organize celebration around chaos, as opposed to cause and effect, we see almost a ubiquitous desire for every moment to become an event in its own right. As we organize our social agenda more around a tribal versus a familial premise, every moment becomes an opportune one for a ritualistic celebration. As the world organizes its affairs around chaos theory and complex adaptive systems, we need reinforcement of the ritualization of "the moment".

> Remember . . . yesterday is but history, tomorrow is a mystery, today is a gift . . . and that is why we call it the present. . . . Our desire is to make every moment an event.

Watts Wacker

when the last deliverable is signed off. Some projects morph and shift rather than truly end – when then is the best time to celebrate?

By all means, throw parties to celebrate the end of something, if that's going to be the best way to say thank you and let off some steam – mankind has been using ritual (rites of passage) to mark transition for aeons.

But don't forget that celebration can be an environment as much as an event. Don't put off into the future what is worth recognizing now. Mark what is happening now. Celebrate effort being made towards results rather than simply results achieved. Celebrate barriers in the process of being broken, rather than just their final elimination. (*Smart Things to Know about Change* for more advice on celebrating achievement and having fun.)

The big point here is that in looking for things to celebrate now, it keeps you in touch with your people.

- They feel that you take the time to know what's going on.

- You *do* know what's going on.

- And any reward you give to people for achieving something (whether it's a pat on the back or a wad of cash) is the best sort of reward in the world – something that is personalized to them. They did something great – you saw it – and you said thank you personally to them...

That in itself is worth celebrating!

SMART QUOTES

> Play defines a culture in ways work never can. Observing how a culture first defines work and then "works" tells us a good deal about the pragmatic aspect of a people: the rules that bind them to each other; the obstacles they face; the challenges they are willing to accept or reject; and their collective ability and will to build toward solution. How a society plays, or individuals inside a society play, gives us a hint of the dreams and nightmares that define people as people.
>
> Ryan Mathews

Now, grab a glass of champagne and we'll move on to the third way that you can ensure that things really get done in your company.

Making things happen 3: minimize confusion and paranoia

People need to know how they are doing.

For years I have seen talented people crumble under the weight of what I can only describe as confusion and paranoia. Although these people have a massive ability to make things happen, without strong feedback on how they are doing they can move in one of two directions, equally dangerous to the organization:

- They can lose confidence – people who are great achievers need to know that what they are doing is having the effect they intend. The most successful people need to be recognized, accepted and approved of.

- They can become loose cannons – achieving, achieving and achieving but all in the wrong direction, because no one was brave enough to harness and coach their energies.

But feedback is an extremely challenging and emotive element of human interaction. It can create tension in both the giver and the receiver – tension which builds before the event, and can linger, adding to the shared filter system, long after it. Why? Because feedback is about telling the truth as you see it. It is about sharing your personal view of the world. in the moments of truth telling, you are no longer part of the crowd, but standing alone, saying "this is my voice".

> The voice emerges literally from the body as a representation of our inner world. It carries our experience from the past, our hopes and fears for the future, the emotional resonance of the moment. If it carries none of these, it must be a masked voice, and having muted the voice, anyone listening knows intuitively we are not all there. Whether or not we try to tell the truth, the very act of speech is courageous because no matter what we say, we are revealed. . . . The voice throws us back on what we want from our life. It forces us to ask ourselves Who is speaking? Who came to work today? Who is working for what? What do I really care about?
>
> David Whyte, *The Heart Aroused*

Giving feedback

I think there are two main categories of feedback. The first is when you want to give someone feedback which is a *recognition* of their achievement. Your intention is that the person leaves this "feedback event" feeling motivated and proud. For this type of communication, there are five main principles:

1. Look like you're about to praise and not kill. Stop scowling for a moment.

2. Make it timely. Not "Do you remember when you rang that client with that piece of product information? That was really good that and I'm ever so pleased. Well done! [Pause] You know. Last August . . .'

3. Make it specific. Not "You're did a really good job in that meeting. Well done!" however well intentioned. What about the good job being done is particularly worthy of praise? Making praise specific highlights what you or the company values. "The way you really listened to what Geoff was saying in that meeting, even though he was blowing his top again – that was really effective. You were able to see exactly what was needed next. Thanks. Well done!"

4. Connect the specific praise to a wider context, whether it be organizational objectives, team goals, the ongoing cultural change effort, your knowledge of the individual's personal development plans . . .

5. Wait a moment. Stay long enough to know that what you have said has sunk in and has been taken in the way you intended it.

The second category of feedback is equally valuable, but perhaps less celebratory. Your intention behind this type is that both parties leave with a greater *understanding* of what happened. Learning happens here. It's the sort of feedback that consultants are trained to give clients (it occasionally happens in the other direction too); you'll need it when you are appraising the progress of a project, reviewing a completed job, or when you need to let an employee know that their performance or behaviour has not reached the required standard.

Here, there are three main principles:

- *Gather all the facts before you open your mouth*
  Other people may have different facts, or versions of facts, which might make the feedback redundant.

- *Feed back facts, not interpretations of facts*
  "The fact is you left the room. My interpretation is that you strongly disagreed with what I was saying and stormed out in an unprofessional manner. But my interpretation is only that – a story I'm telling about reality based on what my filter system allows me to see. What's your interpretation of your leaving the room?"

- *Feed back for improvement and learning, not for fault-assignation*
  What can we do together to improve on this situation? what can we do to make this something that we can learn from? what do both of us have to do to minimize the chances of it happening again?

Performance appraisals

One of the major triumphs of the little known Secret Society for the Bureaucratization and Obfuscation of All Organizations and a finalist in the 1997 "Life's Least Looked Forward to Events" Awards (sponsored by Preparation H), performance appraisals are one of those experiences where both manager and managed are entirely on the same wavelength. In this case both parties are asking the same question: "Isn't there a better way to do this?"

The basic problem with performance appraisals is that they are trying to formalize and time-limit something which is natural and ongoing, i.e. human growth and development. That's tricky in itself. Layered on top of that is the shadow of the school report card which hangs over too many performance appraisals. Someone who is apparently superior to you is going to judge you and tell you whether you're up to the mark. Performance appraisals are a classic business tradition where Shadow 3 managers can reveal themselves – judgemental, backwards-looking, autocratic.

That's going to make things tense for both sides. And yet there's a still further level to the psychological complexity of the drama which is the annual appraisal. Appraisals are supposed to be about the truth. Now, telling and hearing the truth is something that intellectually we have no problem with – it makes perfect sense. Doing it, however, takes us into all manner of emotional minefields, made even worse when the truth teller is someone in (Shadow 3) authority over you.

Perhaps performance appraisals so often fail to achieve their goals because their goals are so complicated. Performance appraisals are supposed to measure you. Fine. They are supposed to demonstrate how much notice the appraiser has been showing towards the appraisee over the time since the last appraisal. Yet they are also supposed to be objective, so trust is going to be a major complicator ("Who is this person to judge me, other than by an accident of hierarchical power relationships?"). They may also be supposed to assess whether you're deserving of a pay rise (but money complicates everything). And they are supposed to set goals for the forthcoming year, or whatever period of time. I'd suggest that the mood and style of a meeting in which you tell someone that they are not going to be able to afford that house move they'd planned is not the same sort of mood and style you'd need for a goal-setting meeting. Something which is supposed to to validate and motivate holds so much potential for demotivation and breakdown of trust.

Measurement is in itself part of the problem. One IT consultancy I know is reappraising its appraisals, because they've found that over the years, everyone if getting 1s and 2s on their corporate standard 5-point grading scale (a 1 is the highest score). This does not make HR happy. What's the point of appraisal if everyone's equally good? Is it an accurate reflection of reality? Furthermore, one person's 2 is another person's 4. I know some perfectionists who'd be crippled by achieving 2 out of 5. Is that their problem or the appraisal system's?

At the same time, performance appraisals have many potential benefits for the organization:

- We need in organizations some way of finding out what's working and what's not. Appraising people regularly is a way for you to generate an understanding of what's happening to the story people are telling about the business, their place in it and its future. What are the themes and patterns emerging from the appraisals you give?

- Appraisals also allow you to generate the next year's training and development plan, one that is centred entirely on real individual and group need.

- They allow you to connect each individual to the organizational strategy, so connecting the micro with the macro. Appraisals should generate a sense not just of individual direction and achievement, but also linkage to the greater good.

. . . and for the individual:

- People definitely need to know if they are on target against the goals they set themselves. Objective feedback is a good way of getting that, since self-perception is a potentially erratic critic. What we think of ourselves and our achievements might be completely twisted by low or high self-esteem, for example.

- People need an outlet for discussing themselves and how they are succeeding rather than just their jobs and activities

- Performance appraisals are also a ritual. No matter how relaxed and informal an organizational culture is, it can benefit from rituals if they are done with the right intentions and in a good spirit. A ritual is a practice designed to generate and hold meaning. In this case, the meaning appraisals are intended to hold is this one: "This organization respects you as an individual, is concerned about your wellbeing, and wants to help you create a powerful plan for your personal development."

Appraisals, like Lucifer, have fallen a long way from their origins, yes?

You have a chance as a manager to exorcize the negative associations of performance appraisals. Forget the once-a-year report card – think ongoing learning events. If need be, co-create with your team or company a different name if "appraisal" has too many negative connotations of an older way of doing things. For me, the following principles should persuade your people that your version of Appraisals is a different order of thing to others they might have experienced. These principles are true if your company calls them appraisals, reviews, feedback meetings, one-on-ones or whatever. I'll leave you to make the choice on title – but for the purposes of this chapter I'll continue to use the term in most common usage: appraisal.

Principles for effective appraisals

1. Remember that an appraisal is a conversation amongst conversations.

My personal development is my responsibility and it occurs over time. My personal development is also partly a function of the quality of conversations I have with my manager and others – the knowledge shared in them, the decisions made and the objectives that are agreed in them. So a conversation/appraisal is a creative form – it creates goals, ambitions, plans and commitments that were not there before. But a conversation/appraisal is also a reflective form. In a healthy organization, I would be used to taking time out from the day to day to reflect on my personal wellbeing and learning – am I moving in the right direction, both for me and for the organization?

That's how you need your people to think – and that's what you need to deliver.

The appraisal is simply a chance to take one further step back from the day to day and look at life and work from the vantage point of a year's passing (or maybe half a year). In just the same way do we set goals every day of our lives – but only feel moved to discuss our New Year's resolutions once a year.

Since both manager and managed are used to using conversation as a creative and reflective form, they will also find that they have strong knowledge to offer when the appraisal happens. In a healthy organization, there are no need for surprises.

The appraisal, then, is an annual ritual (in the strongest, most positive sense of the word) – but actually appraising will have been going on every day in team meetings, one-to-ones, or any time learning is being discussed.

2. Make it understood that the appraisal system is led by your people

and not commanded by you. In effect, the line will be "Hey, manager, I'm going to do my annual Appraisal the week after next – or the week after that – and I'd like you to be there. Which date is good for you?"

3. Before the event, gather information about the person being appraised from their peers, subordinates, clients, customers and any suppliers they work with.

Q: Why do I need to bother with getting others' input into this appraisal? Surely it's just between them and me?

A: Your personal filter system is operating all the time, and especially when you focus on assessing an individual's performance. If they did something eight months ago that really pissed you off, you are likely to let that colour your judgement, thus ignoring the eight months of excellent work since then. Or because they are brilliant at one activity, you ignore other areas in which they are weak. Or simply because you are so damned busy, you unconsciously try to make the individual fit into some safe, simple and preconceived boxes ...

Objective input from outsiders helps make your evaluation accurate and unbiased.

Ask three questions of these people

- What would you like X to do more of?

- What would you like X to do less of?

- What would you like X to keep doing just the same?

4. Encourage your appraisee to ask similar questions of the same people. The person concerned should be appraising themselves – reflecting on their own growth and achievement and needs – rather than just being a passive object of your assessment. How formal and struc-

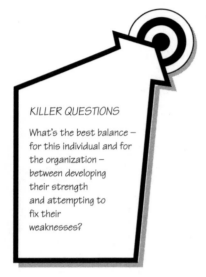

KILLER QUESTIONS

What's the best balance –
for this individual and for
the organization –
between developing
their strength
and attempting to
fix their
weaknesses?

tured you make this "360 degree feedback" approach depends on how trusting you are of your people and how mature and balanced you suspect they are (how likely are they to ask only those people who will be "soft" on them? how likely are they to put negative feedback through their internal filter system?)

5. Your people will ask you for things in these appraisal meetings, so be prepared. They'll ask for career development advice. They'll ask for training. They'll ask you for your formal confirmation of achievement or learning. If they think you haven't done a good enough job of noticing their capabilities in the day to day work, they'll ask for its formal acknowledgement during this conversation.

6. If the subject of targets/goals comes up, encourage people to select their own stretch targets by appealing to their instinct for growth, learning and new experiences. If you set the targets, you may have a tendency to give them targets you know they can achieve – which mean they will always have an unrealistically positive appraisal next time around.

7. Measure only what you/they want to see happen. Measure what you want to create. Offer rewards only for what you and the organization is trying to achieve or express. Reward behaviour in alignment with shared values and objectives rather than solely personal ambition.

8. Discuss not just work done for you and for their project teams – but discuss also their contribution to the mission of the organization. In what ways have they been an excellent corporate citizen as well as a hard worker?

9. Get a single piece of A4 and go to work. Record the date and the place the meeting took place, and a bullet point summary of what was (a) discussed and (b) decided. Both parties should sign the document, not simply to witness that this piece of paper is a fair record of what took place, but also that both parties are making a signed commitment to achieving what is set out therein.

10. Always check that the appraisal meeting met its objectives. Did the appraisee have all his or her concerns met? Are they leaving with their pride intact and their ambitions rekindled?

11. And when will be the next time you think about what's written on that piece of paper? In a few embarrassed hurried moments before next year's meeting? No. Tomorrow. The next time you see the person appraised. Appraisals are rituals, caesuras in the year. Growth and development is ongoing.

12. After the meeting, ask: What can I learn from this conversation? And how am I helping this person?

Removing three major blocks to making things happen

Block 1 – purpose

The question: Is this project not happening because we've lost the plot?

"Lost the plot" is a good metaphor. Think of coming late into a play at the theatre. Or bring to mind a time when, in the midst of watching a two-hour TV drama, you find that you've been day-dreaming for the last 50 minutes. in either case, you'll have had that feeling of important information being missed, seeing clues in front of you but not understanding their significance, not being able to work out the relationship between things and people. That's what working on a project is like when it's lost the plot.

The thing is that in a project no one ever entirely loses the plot – what actually happens is far more dangerous. People, remember, are meaning makers – so if they lose significance, they'll create one. If they can't see a pattern and meaning to events in a project, they'll find it. If they feel things are not properly prioritized, they'll make up prioritization. If they've lost the purpose and final customer for the project, they'll substitute some of their own. Then they'll begin to expend their energies and talents on a project which exists but should not.

The solution: Get back to the source. Step back from activity and hold meetings to examine the project. Don't get stuck at first on "what" questions that create action ("What's gone wrong?" "What should we do next, when and how?") – but start with "why" questions that examine purpose ("Why are we doing this project?" "What are the essential deliverables?" "What isn't this project about?")

An associated problem here is when the project's purpose is out of alignment with that of the organization – it doesn't seem to make sense in the context of the organization's strategy. Get back to the project sponsors or initiators to pick up the threads again.

Block 2 – authority

The question: Who's in charge of making things happen? People are desperate for the acceptance, approval and recognition of others, desperate to make decisions, desperate for a choice, desperate for meaning. Most of those things are provided in business by a leader, someone who demonstrates their freedom by telling them what to do.

The solution: usually comes down to your leadership in four main areas. Firstly, have you appointed a person responsible for each sub. Second, are you acting as a relationship coach – putting people in touch with each other to share knowledge and provide motivation and momentum to each other? Thirdly, are you acting as mentor, being there to give advice? Fourthly, are you being a model for hard work, discipline, learning, honesty and risk-taking?

Block 3 – resources

The question: Have we got the right people together? Do we have the knowl-edge, skills and resources needed to make this project happen? Some projects begin with a level of self-delusion: arrogance, macho attitude or desperation make the project leaders promise impossible deliverables jsut because the organization demands, ought or deserves to have them. I once saw the letters SWATU on a set of internal accounts in a blue chip organization. SWATU was written on the left-hand column, and in the corresponding cell on the spread-sheet it had a fairly sizeable number entered for a month not too far into the future. I was curious, to say the least. So I asked. SWATU, apparently, stands for Something Wonderful Always Turns Up.

The solution: If you don't have what you need, where can you get it? And is the cost of that in alignment with the projected benefits? If not you'll have to defer or delay this project. And learn from it.

When it's not happening like you want it to

A word or two on resistance

Sometimes you'll find that for whatever mysterious reason, despite hav-ing put in place the tools described in this chapter in the spirit in which they are intended, things don't seem to work out as you intend. Spe-cifically, your people seem to resisting your best efforts to take them into the future.

At this point you'll want to label them recalcitrant and irrational.

The word resistance is usually used most in management books in the phrase "resistance to change". Personally I don't believe that people resist change – I think that people hang on to the status quo. This is more than a semantic quibble. People who are exhibiting behaviours that appear to resist the change (i.e. the future) doubt the future. Therefore your leverage point is in explaining and selling the benefits of the future. People who are exhibiting behaviours congruent with holding on to the present/past (i.e. the "status quo') demonstrate a faith in the present/past – so your leverage point is in dismantling that faith.

Furthermore, the very phrase "resistance to change', which has been given by over use such a feeling of gravitas, is practically useless in describing what is actually happening. It's so broad in scope, it's bland, or blind. Resistance to what? To change? In way way? When? To what depth? With what symptoms? Drilling down beyond the phrase "resistance to change", you'll uncover some valuable insights that will lead you to see that people are not resisting change in general, but some very specific things. They may be resisting control. They may be resisting your strategy. They may be resisting conflict. They may be resisting fear. They may well be resisting you.

When you uncover exactly what the person seems to be resisting, you've uncovered your leverage point. If you've found that someone is "resisting change", you've no idea what to do next. If you've found that they're resisting the fear they feel, then you know that you can do something about helping them face and overcome that fear.

Resistance for the purposes of this book means any behaviour that leads you to suspect:

- that you're "not getting through" to your people;

- that although you're getting a "nodding head yes", your intuition tells you that what they really mean is a "shaking head no";

- that there appears to be a disconnect between what they said they'd do and what they'd actually do;

- that you're not convinced about their level of commitment to a task or strategy.

When you feel or sense these things, remember three things about resistance:

1. *Resistance = information.*

Resistance empowers you to solve problems by facing them. If there were no resistance, you might not know you had a problem.

2. *Resistance is a challenge to Shadow 3.*

Shadow 3 tells managers that there is a world where they could be all knowing and all seeing, where they can use their political power to make things happen and get what they want. Resistance is an offence to that world. If you're standing in Shadow 3, casting yourself with a "just do it because I say so" mask, then you are likely to project your "resisting" employees into the role of usurpers/strikers/revolting peasants.

Break down the mythology of Shadow 3. Don't get angry about resistance: get interested in it. What does it tell you? What might be driving it? What is needed next?

3. *Resistance needs to be brought out into the open.*

This sounds judgemental, as if those who are doing the "resisting" are in the wrong. That's not what we intend. After all, your use of the term resistance is a label you put on to a series of behaviours you observe. Who knows who is "right" and what is "true"? Who knows whether the person or people you think are resisting actually intended that by their actions? Who knows if they were even aware how they are behaving? Furthermore, your observation may be skewed by your own filter system – your own attitudes towards power and success, your own conditioning about being right etc. The best way to proceed is to get the resistance out in the open by *talking about it*:

- What precisely do you see and hear that makes you think resistance is occurring?

- Describe this to the people concerned.

- Listen to their response.

4. *Resistance is in your garden too.*

And one final point. As Peter Senge *et al.* point out in *The Dance of Change*, resistance to change is not a rational, planned, intellectual response. Rather it is an emotional, irrational response which in itself is as natural and predictable as are the seasons. Can you imagine your garden if there were only Spring and Summer but no Autumn or Winter? As messy and undesirable as would be an organization where there were no resistance.

Resistance is entirely natural, and is a deeply felt response to the challenges of life. Resistance arises in the human being at that point where he or she knows that they are about to face a real difficulty, problem or complex choice.

Resistance is a sign of growth – and a signal to you that people are on the cusp of success and progress. You'll need your best coaching skills to guide them through these moments. But there is also something else you can do. You can help people to understand that difficulties, problems or complex choices are not a sign that something undesirable is happening, or that something has gone wrong, but are instead the very fabric of life.

In other words, life is difficult.

6

Shit happens

A Smart Thing to Know about People

Life is difficult, and when it shows that it is, people think something has gone wrong. Actually, nothing's gone wrong. It's just life proving that it's difficult.

Here we'll be looking at how you manage the darker side of getting things done: how you and your team can deal with conflict, with communication breakdowns and with shortcomings in performance.

This chapter examines how to deal in a Smart way with those quite normal and natural symptoms that demonstrate life is difficult. In particular we'll look at conflict, difficult conversations, dealing with difficult people and office politics.

For advice on how to deal with the often stressful impact of living in a world of constant change see David Firth, *Smart Things to Know about Change*.

Life is difficult.

This is a great truth, one of the greatest truths. It is a great truth because once we truly see this truth we transcend it. Once we truly know that life is difficult – once we truly understand and accept it – then life is no longer difficult. Because once that is accepted, the fact that life is difficult no longer matters.

Most do not fully see this truth that life is difficult. Instead they moan more or less incessantly, noisily or subtly, about the enormity of their problems, their burdens, and their difficulties as if life were generally easy, as if life should be easy. They voice their belief, noisily or subtly, that their difficulties represent a unique kind of affliction that should not be and that has somehow been especially visited upon them . . . and not upon others. I know about this moaning because I have done my share.

M. Scott Peck, *The Road Less Travelled*

Conflict

The history of humanity is the history of discord, judgement and blame. The history of humanity plays itself out on CNN as I write this. Palestinians fight Israelis, Sierra Leone fights over their choice of leadership and British society argues over what to do with two boys who murdered a toddler eight years ago.

That conflict will arise every day in your organization is as natural and unavoidable as the seasons. The thing is to be unsurprised by it, not hurt by it, and to develop the resolve to tackle it as early as possible. Unresolved conflict festers. We could be throwing stones at each other for decades, long after we've forgotten what the disagreement is really about.

People are strange. They hate the fact that conflict exists – they shrink from confronting it. The man in the pub has just one more pint rather than go home to face the wife he argued with two hours before. The parent worries over whether or not to face up to the child over a disagreement. The employee avoids the conversation with the boss which could solve the problem and mitigate the tension.

And yet, people are strange. They love a good fight. They must do, at some level or other. They certainly seem to be more comfortable with fighting than forgiveness. And why? Because conflict asserts the self. Conflict puts us in touch with our deepest held principles. Conflict makes us feel alive, if only because we're up suddenly up against the possibility of extinction.

Conflict resolution

If you have people who are cursing each other, sending flame mail all having stand up fights in the car park, you should be grateful. At least you know the conflict's there.

By marbling your environment with the regular and varied forms of communication outlined in Chapter 5, you should be able to pick up on tension and conflict that's shimmering in the space between people.

Whether conflict is in your face or under the surface, now is always the time to act.

What do you need to do?

- Address someone's under performance or difficult conduct?

- Challenge the way someone is behaving?

- Deal with an obstructive and destructive colleague?

You'll find advice on what to do in the remainder of this chapter.

But in all situations, you yourself will need to face your own inner conflict: whether or not to open your mouth and say something about the unacceptable situation.

When it's hard to talk: how to engage in difficult conversations

There are many times at work (and just as many in life) when we are faced with the realization that the only thing left to do to improve a situation or solve a problem is to "go and have a word" with someone. When we need ask for a pay rise, or to end a relationship, or to tell someone that their work is not up to scratch, to tell the truth about how we actually feel, even to apologize, we are faced with having a challenging conversation. These conversations are challenging because they demand of us all the skills we have in tact, diplomacy, honesty and creativity. And also because the very anticipation of having them leaves us anxious or even fearful.

Being a good model for challenging conversations – showing that facing up to holding them is a more effective choice for all concerned – helps produce an environment which is characterized by openness and honesty. And it creates an organization where the reality that human beings

Kofi Annan

Kofi Annan was born in Ghana and educated in the US and Europe. A career United Nations diplomat who became Secretary-General in 1997 (the first to be elected from within the organization's ranks), he has, in that role, begun to thrust the UN into new realms of global life. His vision is a policy that calls on the states of the world to step in wherever and whenever human lives are being torn apart by hate, disease or poverty. To guide him, apparently, he follows and advocates the five virtues of his homeland Fante tribe: dignity, confidence, courage, compassion and faith.

do, often, struggle to get on together can be embraced. You will have a workplace where people can "fight gracefully".

Moreover you will have a workplace that moves forwards to the future. Events that trigger the need to have a challenging conversation get frozen in time until that conversation is had. And these frozen moments are not invisible – they are very much present in the minds of the two protagonists, and probably there in the collective mythology of the group. They hang around, festering, haunting the group.

So here are some pieces of advice about having difficult conversations.

[*Note:* The following section is heavily influenced by the wonderfully practical book *Difficult Conversations: How to Discuss what Matters Most* by Douglas Stone, Bruce Patton and Sheila Heen of the Harvard Negotiation Project. Some of this section, however, is not influenced by the book but by my own experience in helping people live and work together in healthy environments. If you don't like anything or disagree violently, blame me and not the authors of *Difficult Conversations*.]

There are times when a difficult conversation is not the best course to take

When your objective is not progress towards the future but revenge or domination, then you should hold back on having the conversation. However:

Avoiding the challenging conversation only makes the situation worse

When you know, deep down, that the only option is to talk, you should arm yourself with the truth that avoiding a challenging conversation is only ever going to make matters worse. At best, avoidance prevents growth, progress or change. If you're lucky.

Unfortunately, the beliefs and emotions existing in any two parties who need to talk do not dissolve or disappear. They grow, nourished by interpretations and stories fed to them by consequent events. Bob and Tony have a big fall out over a failed new business pitch at their agency, accusing each other, variously, of unprofessionalism and misjudgement. After the heat of the initial row has died down, they continue to work together – but in the background of their relationship, each, consciously or subconsciously, looks for more occasions when the other is unprofessional or in error. This relationship is not standing still from not talking: it is spinning away from them. Their positions are hardening – each now convinced they have even more proof that they are "right" and the other is "wrong".

Avoiding the challenging conversation is good for your ego

More than anything, you want the recognition, acceptance and approval of others. That's why you don't like to confront people, challenge them, lay yourself open, be vulnerable. You're scared that will make you "not a nice person". And all your life you try to be a nice person, doing anything that's necessary to keep people from not liking you. Thus does your ego keep you safe from facing, or telling, the truth.

Like most of the ideas in this book, difficult conversations do not work if your only loyalty is to your own agenda

People who face up to having difficult conversations do so because they know that something better than what is occurring now is waiting at the other side of that conversation – a better relationship, maybe, or a truth shared, a request made and considered, an apology accepted. That something better is worth facing their fear for.

Giving up the need to be right, or to win, and taking up the need for a shared solution is critical for the "success" of difficult conversations.

Prepare from reality, not from your mind

False Expectation Appearing Real. FEAR. To keep you from moving forward, your ego will tell you that asking for the rise will cause the boss to sack you, or ridicule you. Your ego will tell you that facing the employee with the truth that their performance at work is now unexpectable will cause them irreparable emotional damage, or will cause them to draw a flick-knife on you, or wipe all the company's hard drives clean.

These possibilities appear real, but are only in your mind. It's a trick you play on yourself.

Prepare for your difficult conversation from reality – from data, data-gathering and reflection on solutions – not from the story you tell yourself about why you can't do what needs to be done.

The tyranny of interpretation: what's your story, morning glory?

This book's messages on communication underline that people are meaning makers. They are addicted to interpretation – they can't allow anything not to mean anything. That's because everything is an interpretation, a story about what has happened, will happen or is happening now.

A conversation is a series of shared stories, proposals and requests. You can't be "right" about the event that's causing you to have this conversation, because that's all that there is. You can however make the story explicit, tell the other person that this is how you arrived at your interpretation of the event, and ask how differently, if at all, they interpreted it.

A detached outsider observing this conversation would also tell what Stone, Patten and Heen describe as the Third Story: "here are two people with disagreement about what happened and what needs to happen". The Third Story – not yours, not theirs, not even a combination of the two – simply expresses that both sides exist and does so without judgement or tension:

Jenny, I know you and I have a big disagreement about what to tell the client on the Nile project. My sense is that we should do ABC, but from

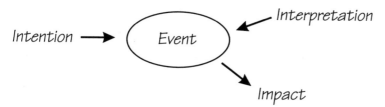

Figure 6.1

what I've seen you do and say in the past – DEFG – I'm guessing that you want to do HIJK. Maybe together we can sort out why we feel so differently about this situation and figure out what to do about it?

Stepping in to the Third Story includes both perspectives and invites joint participation towards a shared solution.

As well as explaining how you got to your interpretation, inquiring into how they got to theirs, and looking for the Third Story that encompasses your conversation, you can also explain your intentions behind the Event.

Exploring the intent/impact misalignment

Every event has an intention. Every event also has a story or interpretation constructed about it. Every event also has an impact, which might or might not be the one intended (Figure 6.1).

Breakdown in communication comes when:

1. people mistake their interpretation of the Event with the only possible interpretation, or with Absolute Truth

and

2. people assume they know each other's intentions without actually asking what they are.

A manager at a call centre which was plagued by low morale and mistrust of management once gave her staff an alarm clock. Her Intention was to encourage her staff not to spend too long taking abuse from the very many dissatisfied callers that the company had – but to divert calls to her or another senior staff member.

KILLER QUESTIONS

What voices are not being heard here in all these disagreements?

The Interpretation that soon was shared as truth by the staff was that the manager intended to make callers work faster, and take more calls per hour. This Interpretation was fuelled by the collective filter model that this team had set up about how management treated them in this company.

The Impact was greater mistrust, anger and resentment.

The gap between Intention and Impact is what needs to be discussed in any difficult conversation.

[I have no doubt that the manager concerned actually did explain her intention when she gave the team the clock. Maybe she didn't explain it well or strongly enough to counter the filtering process already going on in her team. Maybe it's true that people don't like reality to get in the way of a good story.]

Be truthful about the impact of the Event on you and how that makes you feel

Your interpretation can never be right (though it might, in the end, be accepted or even shared), but sentences that begin "I feel..." can never be wrong.

Blame does not solve, but it is a powerful sign

Blame, judgment, generalizations and accusations are indications that the two parties have moved away from a position of seeking shared solutions to one of defence and attack ("I am right and you are wrong'). When these behaviours crop up, move back to the Third Story.

Take responsibility for your part in the Impact

Blame also occurs when a hurt person wants someone else to take some responsibility for how they feel – and take some of the hurt away. You can never be responsible for someone else's feelings or interpretation, but you can take responsibility for your part in creating the Impact. The manager with the clock can accept that her actions could be misconstrued, and that by not checking that her Intention was clear, that she contributed to the problem.

> Before you even begin a difficult conversation, no matter how strongly you feel that someone else was wrong or needs to change, ask: *"What did I contribute to this problem?"*

KILLER
QUESTIONS

Dalai Lama

The Dalai Lamas are the manifestations of the Bodhisattva (Buddha) of Compassion, who chose to reincarnate to serve the people.

His Holiness the 14th the Dalai Lama Tenzin Gyatso is the head of state and spiritual leader of the Tibetan people. He was born Lhamo Dhondrub on 6 July 1935, in a small village called Taktser in northeastern Tibet. Born to a peasant family, he was recognized at the age of two, in accordance with Tibetan tradition, as the reincarnation of his predecessor, the 13th Dalai Lama, and thus an incarnation of Avalokitesvara, the Buddha of Compassion.

On 17 November 1950, he was called upon to assume full political power (head of state and government) after some 80,000 People's Liberation Army soldiers invaded Tibet. In 1954, he went to Beijing to talk peace with Mao Tse-tung and other Chinese leaders, including Chou En-lai and Deng Xiaoping. His efforts to bring about a peaceful solution to Sino-Tibetan conflict were thwarted by Bejing's ruthless policy in eastern Tibet, which ignited a popular uprising and resistance. The Tibetan uprising was brutally crushed by the Chinese army. The Dalai Lama escaped to India where he was given political asylum. Some 80,000 Tibetan refugees followed His Holiness into exile. Today, there are more than 120,000 Tibetans live there in exile.

The Norwegian Nobel Committee's decision to award the 1989 Peace Prize to His Holiness the Dalai Lama won worldwide praise and applause, with the exception of China. The Committee's citation read, "The Committee wants to emphasize the fact that the Dalai Lama in his struggle for the liberation of Tibet consistently has opposed the use of violence. He has instead advocated peaceful solutions based upon tolerance and mutual respect in order to preserve the historical and cultural heritage of his people."

On 10 December 1989, His Holiness accepted the prize on the behalf of oppressed everywhere and all those who struggle for freedom and work for world peace and the people of Tibet. In his remarks he said, "The prize reaffirms our conviction that with truth, courage and determination as our weapons, Tibet will be liberated. Our struggle must remain nonviolent and free of hatred."

www.tibet.com – the Office of Tibet, the official agency of His Holiness the Dalai Lama in London

Balance curiosity and listening, inquiry and advocacy

Listen to understand the other's perspective on what happened. Ask questions. Summarize it to show you're listening and to check that you're getting it right. Acknowledge expressions of feelings, or admissions of contribution. Acknowledge too when you feel that the other has just stepped way outside their comfort zone to say a particular thing. Recognize their risk-taking or fear-facing.

> If we can learn to put away fear and anger and sadness and judging and, instead, fill our hearts with joy, the Spirit will be indwelling with us and will guide our thoughts and moods and actions and we will have a better world much faster than if we lecture each other sternly about our perceptions of each other's failings.
>
> Father Teilhard de Chardin

Allow silence

Difficult conversations need time for perspectives to shift and for emotions to be calmed.

SWYM

Say what you mean, and mean what you say. Speak to what matters most.

Keep trying

Stay long enough to move beyond the expressions of anger, confusion or hurt

King Solomon

King David's son, Solomon, inherited a unified prosperous kingdom. Building on David's achievements, Solomon established an efficient centralized government, with a professional army and an advanced trade network. Above all, he lavished attention on Jerusalem, raising splendid public buildings and palaces, and carrying out his father's plan to erect a temple worthy to house the Ark of the Covenant. The temple was a most spectacular and expensive construction project; the walls, the ceiling, even the floors were all covered with gold. Lavishness, evidently, was his forte in more ways than one. Solomon had 700 wives and 300 concubines. Many of the exotic women were in fact living treaties: he maintained alliances by taking wives from the family of every potentate willing to sign a compact. He even kept Egypt out of Israel by marrying an Egyptian princess, the daughter of a pharaoh. Talk about giving it up for the job.

But it is for his wisdom that Solomon is most revered. He once threatened to cut a baby in half, which had the effect of focusing the two debating mothers marvellously on the truth and on their consciences. The one who was the real mother offered to give her baby away to the other, in order to save its life, thus revealing her true love for the child. Shit happens, and still people strive to do good.

Keep making requests and promises:

- Request that the other person work with you towards solution.

- Promise behaviour that will help that process.

- Promise what is needed to bring about the solution that satisfies both parties.

- Request that we have review points and that we keeping talking . . .

Challenging gracefully

Challenging the status quo

- Speak from your personal experience.

- Don't attach meaning/significance to events which are only your own.

- Promote understanding above advice: for every "what" try to come up with at least two "whys'".

- Consider and take responsibility for what part you have played in creating the situation.

- Speak to the future (seek to be constructive, positive and solution-oriented) rather than the past.

Q: You'll never make all the people get on with all the people all of the time, will you?

A: No; but interpersonal differences can lead people to neglect shared vision and responsibility – and that neglect needs facing.

SMART
ANSWERS
TO TOUGH
QUESTIONS

Challenging Generalizations in Colleagues' Conversations

For example, "Nothing ever changes . . ." "They always get it wrong . . .'

- Clarify what actually happened – ask precision questions: eg "what exactly doesn't change?" Do we have the facts? What evidence is there to back up your opinion?

- Change perspective – would an objective outsider be able to make the same observation?

- Challenge – would they say the same thing, in the same way, to their boss? If not, how would it be different?

- Encourage ownership – offer advice on who the person should see with their opinion . . .

Confronting underperformance or ill-discipline

- Be compassionate first of all

    - this does not mean forgive stupidity or misdeed; it means strive to understand the context for the problem

- Don't rush

    - take care not to judge too soon; check the intrusion of your personal filter systems

- Be current

    - discipline as soon after the event as possible

- Be fair

    - apply discipline consistently

- You can always shout and scream later

    - start with the least severe action that will rectify the performance

- Focus on performance not personality

Dealing with difficult people

Some people are the way they are because they are the way they are – and all your powers of influence can't change them. Here are four such types of difficult people – and some tips on how to deal with them:

Sherman tanks: they state opinions as facts and try to intimidate you with in-your-face arguments

- Get their attention by using their first name to begin a sentence.

- Maintain eye contact; give them time to wind down.

- Stand up to them without fighting; don't worry about being polite.

- Suggest you sit down to continue talking.

Snipers: take potshots in meetings but avoid one-on-one confrontations.

- Expose the attack; draw them out in public and don't let social convention stop you.

- Get other opinions. Don't give in to the sniper's views.

- Provide the sniper with alternatives to a direct contest.

Chronic complainers: they find fault with everyone – except themselves.

- Politely interrupt and get control of the situation.

- Quickly sum up the facts.

- Ask for their complaints in writing.

Negativists: they just know that nothing new will work; they'll suck the energy out of your best proposals.

- Acknowledge their valid points; ignore the rest.

- Describe past successes.

- Avoid "You're wrong, I'm right" arguments.

Exploders: they throw tantrums that can escalate quickly.

- Give them time to regain self-control.

- If they don't, shout a neutral phrase such as "Stop!"

- Take a time-out or have a private meeting with them.

Robert Bramson, *Coping with Difficult People*

– you can change one but not the other

• Before the conversation for change:

– learn: ask what part you have played in this person's under performance

• When facing the situation, have the conversation for change:

– describe the facts

– describe the impact of these facts on the overall team/company objectives

– check for understanding (do these facts have a different interpretation from their point of view?)

– describe the changes you need to observe, the goal you're looking for

– describe the checks and controls that you'll put in place to support the change

– check for willingness to comply with the change

– ask for commitment

– offer any help necessary (including training)

Office politics

At the heart of the human experience is a great loneliness and isolation which people attempt to overcome by working and living together in groups. People seek affinity and connection with others.

Also at the heart of the human experience is a great insecurity, which people attempt to overcome by winning, or at least not losing. People seek domination over others, or they seek to avoid domination.

Put those two strategies and you get office politics . . .

Or at least you get the dark side of office politics, the pursuit of personal agendae in spite of – or sometimes at the expense of – other people or organization's aims.

- When people practice cover-their-arse behaviour (e.g. cc'ing everyone and his dog into emails just to demonstrate "Look, I've done this!")

- When people bypass "traditional" communication channels or subvert agreed ways of operating

- When people say yes but mean maybe, or maybe and mean no

Is this behaviour wrong? Should people be punished for it? No. It's a normal human expression of power exchange – I try to make something happen, I ask for your support and at the same time I try to protect myself.

Organizations from this angle are a complex of dependencies.

And office politics is also entirely understandable and inevitable because people in organizations have different spheres of influence – and they have different perceived spheres of influence – not always congruent with their job title or position in the hierarchy. If I think you can get something done, I'll come to you and make a request (and an offer in return).

So when is office politics damaging – and what can you do about it?

First, try imagining that you'd never heard of the phrase "office politics" or the concept it signifies. What would you see? You'd see people trying to make things happen – which is a great thing, isn't it. And you'd see, sometimes, people acting selfishly, which may be regrettable depending on your personal value system, but hardly the most surprising thing you'll ever experience. They'll do things which you perceive as underhand, even devious, and that will annoy you (as if human beings were angels....). What if the deviousness produced exceptional results? Do you praise the ends and condemn the means? Why would you do that?

There are two times that "office politics" is truly a problem, and on both occasions its a problem because it disables the organization rather than offends your personal value system.

The first is when trust is damaged.

Trust is a precious commodity, the oxygen of a healthy and learning organization. It cannot be abused with impunity.

Michael Hammer – advocate or villain?

I remember hearing a tape of Hammer speaking back in about 1993 (it was a bootleg of a business conference, no less – I have some sad friends) and being blown away by his humour, energy and style. In particular, I recall a description he made of a process-driven organization where people were motivated to help each other, because such intimate connection is central to human nature "and human nature" he said, "lies at the centre of the process organization".

And yet, and yet . . . Michael Hammer was the co-author of the book *Reengineering the Corporation* and the patriarch of Business Process Reengineering, a methodology so powerful that it persuaded hundreds of organizations worldwide to lay off thousands upon thousands of workers. Mention Michael Hammer now in some parts of the US and they'll spit in your face. Reengineering, for them, means layoffs, downsizing, rightsizing, redundancies, early retirement, bitterness, anger, despair. Who said gurus don't really change anything?

Reengineering traces its origin to the period in the 1980s when many large organizations suddenly awoke to the need for drastic improvement. In every measurable way, companies were letting their customers down. They were slow to respond, they were inflexible, they made stupid errors – and they charged their customers a lot for this service. People were focused on doing a good job in their particular area or function, and cared little for what was happening in the area or function next door, still less for a distant and anonymous customer. Reengineering shifts the organization out of this narrow, internal focus to looking at the larger picture which is the business process (input in, output out; raw materials in at one end, satisfied customer out at the other).

In a non-reengineered organization, people are made to look stupid or lazy or incompetent because of the number of mistakes, hand-offs, recycling of errors, and the slowness and unpredictability with which the customer gets served (Waste, Hammer once said, is "marbled in" to organizations). Hammer's assertion is that all this is not in fact the people's fault, but the process's fault – and thus qualifies for his Pro-Human Award.

And yet, and yet . . . the central paradox of Hammer's influence is that the efficiencies he promised through the potential of reengineering (potential being

*SMART
PEOPLE
TO HAVE
ON YOUR
SIDE*

the operative word since up to 70% of reengineering efforts apparently fail) could only ever be truly delivered by cutting the number of people in organizations.

So is the world a better or a worse place for Michael Hammer?

Is Michael Hammer a story about reengineering at all? Or about the difficulty – and dangers – of applying theory in practice? Is it about business people and their relationship to business gurus? Is it about the human need to believe that something wonderful is always on offer? Or the fact that sometimes in life, shit happens?

When an individual takes action which causes people not just to mistrust him or her but also each other – ie when the team lapses into paranoia – then that's a time to take action to repair the trust. It might mean the individual concerned simply explaining their actions, giving the context and intention behind the behaviour. It might mean the individual apologizing.

The second time that "office politics" is a problem is when the greater good suffers.

Any attempt to seize personal power that does not contribute to the shared purpose of the organization is bound to have negative outcomes for all concerned. Healthy organizations do not allow individuals to harm themselves for the sake of the company – that is why they are so concerned with personal well-being, the impact of stress, the dangers of urgency-addiction and the realities of work/life balance. Healthy organizations similarly do not allow the greater good to be harmed for the sake of one person's ego.

7

Embracing the future

A Smart Thing to Know about People

People operate in the present to the future they believe they have available to them.

In this chapter, we'll be looking at how you can keep the future fresh and compelling for your people.

I got it, once and for all, at a three-day seminar at the end of the last century. Big room, white walls, aircon machine droning, rows of delegates facing front, listening to Jacques, or Jean, or Filbert, French guy anyway, powerful voice, many cigarettes in his past, playing up his accent, ahawhehaw.

The guy said "I'm going to say something outrageous" (*"outrageous"* said almost appalled, growls it out almost onomatopoeically, in the way John Cleese says it in that Monty Python sketch).

We look up from out notebooks. All of us. He's going to say something outrageous. Well, with a promise like that, you're at least going to lend an ear, right?

"Human beings (*"uman beens"*) are not a product of their past."

I'm not alone, in that room at the end of the last century, to be surprised at what he said. I guess you are too. Most of this book has asserted that people live in the past, where they are held by the old ideas, assumptions and beliefs they've had about such things as work, bosses, performance appraisals.

I was more than surprised, though. More than that, I found Jacques' (or Jean's, or Filbert's) assertion, well, how he said it would be: *outrageous...*

Yet he had more to say.

"Who you are in the present is given only be the future you have to live into.

Why it seems that we are products of our past is that our future is our past."

I was amazed. What's the guy talking about? We haven't even had the future yet – how can it be already in our past.

And he was right.

Think about it. There you are on a Friday evening, 5.30 p.m., just replying to a few final emails, making sure the desk is clear for the Monday morning, closing a call from a supplier, asking about their plans for the weekend, making appropriate facial gestures to the colleague standing with his coat on in the doorway to indicate that yes you will be coming for a pint at the Dog, because why, because

> *It's the Weekend!!*

and how do you feel

> *I feel fantastic!!*

and why do you feel fantastic?

> *Because it's the Weekend!!!*

And where is the weekend?

> *It's here!*

Actually no . . .

OK then, it's coming, it's in the very near future, it starts as soon as I walk out of that door . . .

Well, yes in a sense, you're right. The future promised by this weekend is making you feel great.

But in fact this future is fed by the past – by all your experiences of weekends in the past, with all their leisure and pleasure and fun and freedom. So the past is in your future, your future is your past.

Hmmm. OK. So what? I still feel great. That's not bad is it?

Not at all. The future you have to live into, the one that the past has fed you with its backlog of leisure and pleasure and fun and freedom, doesn't disempower you.

But consider: how will you be feeling on Sunday night, at about 9 p.m.?

A little bit tense about going back to work; I'll be starting to think of everything I've got to do on Monday morning, about that nasty deadline on the Abilene project. About that meeting I have with my boss to explain why we're over budget. Then I'll find it difficult to concentrate on the remaining hours of my weekend . . .

And where does those feelings come from? From the future of Monday mornings . . .

. . . which is fed by all my past of Monday mornings . . .
I get it . . .

And in that case your past, which is waiting for you again in your future, does disable you, does disempower you, because it leaves you tense and anxious in the present.

What's the implication for you as a manager? There are two.

The first is to get clear on the past and leave it there. This means having the capacity to face every new challenge as if it were a new one, so that you take from the past everything that will help you (e.g. learning, knowledge, experience) and leave behind that which will disempower you (e.g. stress, anxiety, worry, fear).

SMART QUOTES

"The future belongs to those who prepare for it today."
Malcolm X

The second is to set a future for your workforce that continually refreshes and inspires them. There is something about work, about even the best organizations, which is repetitious and mundane. We come to the same place every day – no matter how jazzily decorated that place is, it's the same one as yesterday. We work with the same people every day – no matter how clear our communications are, not matter how rich our relationships, they're the same people as yesterday. The past is having a chance to travel into the future.

Smart things to say

I want my people to say "Hey great it's the weekend!" And I also want them to say on a Monday morning "Hey, great, it's work today!"

So here are numerous ways, some profound, some funny, all meant to be taken seriously, to make the future of your workplace more compelling than its past.

Fight for integrity

Get people to stand up for what they promise or say that they will do or commit to. There's nothing wrong with changing our minds or for making mistakes. But not owning up to our mistakes, covering them up, adding a white lie to a half-truth in order to cover our backs, all that undermines the foundations of a truly great workforce. Take responsibility for your mistakes, apologise unreservedly for your breaches in integrity – and demand others do the same.

SMART QUOTES

"Opportunities multiply as they are seized."

Sun-Tzu

Fight for community

Call people towards the greater good of the whole, call them away from

working towards their personal agendae. Ask them who benefits from their decision, their action or their words – apart from them. In this way, connect individual action to universal results

Sort out who your enemy is

And it's rarely who you think it is. It's not senior management, it's not the customer, it's not the users, it's not them.

Generate facemail rather than email

We have (in most of the world) the apparent ubiquity of communications devices and the emergence of the first true global language on the horizon. I believe all of this will cause us to thirst for even more direct face-to-face and body-cue language than ever before. Some of the earliest research works on the nature of people's communication on the Internet indicates that individuals who develop a relationship "in the ether" have an incredible desire for face-to-face contact. That face-to-face component of their communication may be less frequent than in the "meat world" but that doesn't mean our need for it will go away.

Watts Wacker

Mix up jobs

Get people to engage in the work that others in the company do, so that

they build perspectives on others' challenges and problems. In
turn this will reduce their willingness to believe that the grass is
always greener on the other side.

Mix up customers

Get them in to tell all levels of your people stories of what it's
like to be served by your company. This is not just a job for an
objective report from a consultant, where what your customers
think and feel is sanitized, summarized and bullet-pointed. One of the
most powerful corporate events I've ever attended was one where a Big
Airline was addressed by a prospective Airline Alliance partner and told
just what it was like to work alongside them. A couple of AA stories
were more insightful and shocking than a hundred Powerpoint slides.

Understand the lettuce

When you plant lettuce, if it does not grow well you don't blame the
lettuce. You look for reasons it is not doing well. It may need fertil-
izer, or more water, or less sun. You never blame the lettuce.

Yet if we have problems with our friends or our family, we blame
the other person. But if we know how to take care of them, they will
grow well, like the lettuce. Blaming has no positive effect at all, nor
does trying to persuade using reason and arguments.

That is my experience.

No blame, no reasoning, no argument, just understanding.

If you understand, and you show that you understand, you can
love, and the situation will change.

Thich Nhat Hahn

Mix up customers 2

Invite your customers to tell stories to each other. Ask for a transcript or a copy.

Decrease the competitiveness of the environment

Competition discourages change. Desperate to please whoever is judging the competition (i.e. you), people will keep playing the same games. The status quo is reinforced.

A hope deferred make the something sick

It has always been the way of things that people want their needs satisfied. What they don't realize, when they ask for these needs to be satisfied, is how absolutely delighted they'll be if their expectations are not just met, but surpassed. Challenge your people to see "surpassing the need" as your own expectation of quality. "The customer wants X? How could we give X+?" Eventually, you're people will cotton on that there's an expectation to surpass your own need, your own expectation . . .

Be a storyteller and a storycollecter

When people gather together they tell stories. They can't help it, because from one perspective, it's all a story, it's all made up. Events? – whooooosh – gone! Happened. Never to return. All that's left is the stories we tell each other about what happened. The stories your group tells about your company and how it works give meaning to the past and provide a context for the present. Your job is to know what those meanings are, because if they are stories are disabling, negative, destructive, warped, then it's a sign that your group is going to struggle stepping into the future. Your job is also to tell stories that *move* people . . . into the future.

> Q: Why worry about tomorrow, when the only time I can act is today?
>
> A: Because your actions today create certain possible futures – and obliterate all the rest. Don't try to create a desired future one step at a time. Imagine the desired future – with clarity and passion – and work backwards into today.

SMART
ANSWERS
TO TOUGH
QUESTIONS

Change the language

What does the word competition mean to you and your colleagues? Danger? Attack? Scarcity? Enemy? War? What impact might it have on how people worked if competitors were known as "alternatives"? Similarly, is it right in these days of Brand of You and Free Agent Nation to still be using the term "employee"? And is "manage" what you do?

People make words mean stuff, and those meanings can constrain their behaviour.

Ban clipart

Get someone from IT to eradicate the clipart libraries from everyone's machines. There is nothing more dead than a bunch

KILLER QUESTIONS

What did we say
we'd do today?

of iconography designed 20 years ago to make "busy executives" of 15 years ago more "fun". If I see one more Powerpoint slide titled "The Contract" or "The Agreement" with that clipart drawing of two hands shaking, I'm going to reach for my gun. And the same goes for that one of the old guy with a balding head punching his fist into his palm out of frustration or because he's just made a great decision or something.

Expect growth and development (or whatever) and you'll get it

Expect is from Latin words which mean "to draw forth". Expecting is not passive but active. Talent is absolutely dependent on the willingness and innate abilities of the person. Talent is also also absolutely dependent on your capacity for encouraging it to show and develop.

Post up the following

The Six Mistakes of Man

1. The delusion that personal gain is made by crushing others.

2. The tendency to worry about things that cannot be changed or corrected.

3. Insisting that a thing is impossible because we cannot accomplish it.

4. Refusing to set aside trivial preferences.

5. Neglecting development and refinement of mind, and not acquiring the habit of reading and studying.

6. Attempting to compel others to believe and live as we do.

Cicero

KILLER QUESTIONS
What did we do
that we didn't
think we'd do?

Be a change agent

Enterprises are like the environment, or the weather, or the economy . . . they are open, interactive, complex, adaptive, self-organizing, nonlinear, dynamic, emergent and playful.

The first underlying principle of the Xerox Business Services change strategy was to disturb the system simultaneously all over the place – in big ways and small, individually and collectively.

The second was to disturb it in ways congruent with the kind of organization we wanted to create.

The third was to invite participation not to insist or enforce it.

The fourth was to design many offerings so that people could choose how to participate.

KILLER QUESTIONS
What have we
learnt for
tomorrow?

The fifth was to keep the strategy loose, improvisational and experimental so that we could learn along the way.

Margaret Wheatley

Margaret J. Wheatley is a consultant, speaker and the best-selling author of *Leadership and the New Science: Discovering Order in a Chaotic World* and *A Simpler Way* (with M. Kellner-Rogers). She is president of the Berkana Institute, a non-profit educational and scientific research foundation supporting the discovery of new organizational forms. She is also a principal of Kellner-Rogers & Wheatley, Inc., a consulting firm that focuses on applying natural science principles in self-organization that engage the intelligence of the entire organization to respond to change continuously.

> *Leadership and the New Science* was originally published in 1992, critics hailed it as a ground breaking work. It provided a unique interpretation of the emerging "new science" and how its concepts apply to organizations, leadership, and change. . . . Using explanations and examples derived from quantum physics and chaos theory, Wheatley asserts that organizations are not machines that can be regulated through planning, procedures, power, or control. Rather they are living organisms that, when given plenty of trust and freedom and inspiring leadership, can creatively adapt to changing times. Information flowing freely throughout the system is the energy source – the catalyst for intelligent change. In self-renewing cycles, energies and eddies feed back upon themselves into new structures and solutions. The more open a system is to new information, both from within and out, the more creative its adaptations. The patterns of relationships, and the capabilities available to form them in these living systems, become critical—not its hierarchies, tasks, and functions.
>
> from a review of *Leadership and the New Science* by Beth Garlington Scofield

Margaret Wheatley challenges some of our most fundamental beliefs about the way the world works:

> I realized that I and others weren't asking people simply to adopt some new approaches to leadership, or to think about organizations in a few new ways. What we were really asking, and what was also being asked of us, was that we change our thinking at the most fundamental level, that of our world view. The dominant worldview of Western culture – the world as

machine – doesn't help us to live well in this world any longer. We have to see the world differently if we are to live in it more harmoniously.

Some organizations, says Wheatley are beginning to eliminate "rigidity, both physical and psychological, in order to support more fluid processes whereby temporary teams are created to deal with specific and ever-changing needs. They have simplified roles into minimal categories; they have knocked down walls and created workplaces where people, ideas, and information circulate freely."

At the centre of this work is a profound respect for the individual (one of her essays is called "Remembering Human Goodness"), even though the new sciences urge us to remember that the only material form is that of relationships, and in truth there is no sense of an individual that exists independent of its relationships. The emphasis therefore is on the health of the environment, which either enables or disables connection:

> Life is creative. It makes it up as it goes along, changing the rules even. This behaviour flies in the face of the logic we inherited about how the world worked. Most of us grew up in world where we believed things existed in a fixed and independent state. Things could be understood by analysis. Laws and principles could be extracted from observations of their behaviour. Predictions could be made for similar situations. Right answers would be won by bright minds. Safety would be earned by assiduous analysis.
>
> We have focused for a long time on trying to discover what's right. We have taken things apart, sifting through our analysis for the right answer, creating more and more debris, surrounded by numbers that overwhelm us with dissatisfactions.
>
> These activities are cloaked in terror. What if we don't find it? What if we get it wrong? What if someone else finds it before we do? Extinction will follow swiftly on the heels of any mistake. This fear of error seems the darkest of Darwinian shadows. When errors hold so much peril, play disappears. Creativity ceases. Only fear and struggle persist. Paradoxically, we make greater errors.
>
> We say to one another, "Get it right first time." How can we live with so much fear?
>
> *A Simpler Way*

The sixth was to go to fertile ground – to offer our help and support to those who really wanted it.

The seventh principle recognized that it doesn't take 100% of the organization's people to change a system. After all, fewer than 3% of Americans fought in the Revolution.

And the eighth principle was to let go of outcomes. There's some evidence that hard-and-fast objectives actually limit the possibilities.

(Adapted from Chris Turner, *All Hat and No Cattle: Shaking Up the System and Making a Difference at Work*)

Know when to get out

If you haven't struck oil, stop boring.

Further reading

We don't receive wisdom; we must discover it for ourselves after a journey that no one can take for us or spare us.

Marcel Proust

And yet, many people act as signposts along the way.

Here is a list of books by people who have profoundly influenced my thinking on the human being at work and beyond it. This page is just a small way of my giving thanks to these people – and a chance for me to commend them to you.

Block, Peter, *Flawless Consulting*, Jossey-Bass.
Chowdhury, S. (ed.), *Management 21C: Some Day We'll All Manage this Way*, Financial Times/Prentice Hall.
Godz, K. (ed.), *Community Building*, New Leaders Press.
Handy, Charles, *The Empty Raincoat, The Hungry Spirit*, Hutchinson.
Isaacs, William, *Dialogue*, Currency Doubleday.
Moore, Thomas, *Care of the Soul*, Harper.
Owen, Harrison, *Open Space Technology*, Berrett-Koehler

Scott Peck, M., *The Road Less Travelled and Beyond*, Rider.

Senge, Peter, *The Dance of Change, The Fifth Discipline Fieldbook*, Brearley.

Stanfield, R. Brian, *The Courage to Lead*, New Society Publishers.

Walsch, Neale Donald, *The Conversations with God* series, Hodder and Stoughton.

Wheatley and Kellner-Rogers, *A Simpler Way*, Berrett-Koehler.

Whyte, David, *The Heart Aroused*, Currency Doubleday.

Zukav, Gary, *The Seat of the Soul*, Rider.

And the work both of Matthew Fox and Landmark Education

Index